*Blissful Kids*

ULTIMATE MINDFULNESS ACTIVITY BOOK

150 Playful Mindfulness Activities for Kids and Teens (and Grown-Ups too!)

BY CHRISTIAN BERGSTROM

Cover illustration by Ayelen Lamas

ISBN-13: 978-952-94-0769-9

www.blissfulkids.com/books/

For orders, visit www.blissfulkids.com/orders/

ISBN: 978-9-52940-769-9

DEDICATION

This book is dedicated to my two miracles,
my son, Anton, and my wife, Hanna.

I love you so much!

<3 <3 <3

.

ACKNOWLEDGMENTS & GRATITUDE

A humble thank you to my two amazing editors, Trelani Duncan and Annie Mahon. Thank you so much for improving this book! Many wonderful people have helped me create this book. I could never have accomplished this book without you. Thank you for your support, hard work, and gracious help. Holly Parker, Angel Woodard, Blair Buttler, Prudence Tippins, Jessica Allowski, Michelle Paget, Erika Krull, and Celia Speirs. Thanks for your support and for helping making this book great!

And... hugs to all the wonderful people who have sent in activities. Keep sending them in so that we can share more mindfulness with the rest of the world—in this book and on our blog. And many thanks to the ingenious people who have created and developed activities. If you are one of those, please let me know so that I can give you a shout-out in a future edition of this book. My one regret with this book is that I haven't been able to mention all the people who have created and further developed these fantastic mindfulness activities. I wish to do so in the future.

Finally, thank *you*—the reader. By buying this book, you help share mindfulness, and we get to write more books and publish more mindfulness activities on our blog free for everyone. Most importantly, by practicing with your kids, you are building a better world! Yay, you :-)

With much gratitude and appreciation,
Chris Bergstrom

DOWNLOAD AUDIO
COURSE FOR FREE

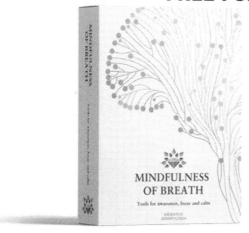

$79 FREE FOR YOU!

Read This First!

Free audio course for you—valued at $79!

Just to say thanks for buying my book, I would like to give you a guided mindfulness course 100% FREE!

TO DOWNLOAD GO TO: www.blissfulkids.com/book-vip/

CONTENTS

CHAPTER 1

INTRODUCTION

Congrats!

The fact that you are reading this book right now and planning to practice with your kids is reason enough to celebrate.

Yay, you!

Picture me doing a goofy fist pump here :-) Seriously, you are giving your kids and yourself a beautiful gift. And by practicing with the kids, you are contributing to a better world!

A Letter to You from Chris

Hi! I'm Chris. I'm a dad, and I teach mindfulness to kids, teens, and grown-ups. As a parent, I'd do anything to see my son grow up healthy and happy. We want our children to flourish, it's only natural. What if there was a way to set your child up for more joy and kindness and less stress and negativity? What if you could give your kid lasting life skills to de-stress and calm down, navigate difficult emotions, control impulses, focus on what matters, and nurture empathy, kindness, and positivity? The good news is that with mindfulness practice, you can nurture all of those skills... And the book you are holding is packed with activities to develop these exact skills.

My four-year-old son Anton already knows that he has concrete tools to help him be focused, calmer, less scared, and happier when he needs to be. He even knows how to cheer *me* up by gently guiding me through a joy-boosting gratitude practice. Anton does that when he sees that I'm feeling down. It's amazing what kids can do!

Kudos to you for being willing to take time to nurture yourself and your loved ones. I sincerely want you to reap the same kind of rewards that I've enjoyed. I want to give you easy access to that same sense of contentment, accomplishment, and connection with your kids.

I practice mindfulness because it makes me a kinder, calmer, happier, and more balanced dad. I practice with my son Anton so that he can cultivate kindness and empathy – and be more accepting of himself and others. So that he can deal with difficult emotions and find joy and happiness every single day, even when life gets intense.

Mindfulness activities help grown-ups, children, teens, and whole families. It's amazing how we can bring about positive change with tiny little steps. Simple and short activities, when repeated, have the power to change our lives for the better.

This book is filled with tried and true activities for both kids and teens... not theory. To boot, I put together a list of actionable advice in the form of best practices. By following this advice, you can soon start and sustain a successful mindfulness practice with your kids.

In my opinion, introducing mindfulness to your kids is one the greatest gifts you can offer. Start practicing mindfulness today, and take your kids on a rewarding adventure. I wish you a wonderful time together!

Chris Bergstrom,
Chief Mindfulness Ninja at BlissfulKids.com

PS
If, after reading this book, you feel like you'd like me to show you step-by-step how to integrate mindfulness into your routines at home (or at school) in a sustainable way, I recommend you join one of our online courses. I'd be happy to have you onboard! You can check our offering here: www.blissfulkids.com/courses/

How to Use This Book

This book is easy to use. The activities in this book will allow you to integrate mindfulness into your lives in a playful and practical way. Most activities can be individualized to meet a specific kid or family's needs. In other words, you can modify them to fit your kid's age and maturity. I have divided 150+ mindfulness activities into three categories to help you choose activities that will best support you and your kids.

Activities for sensory awareness, focus, and calm
Experiment with simple and playful activities that work for almost any age. These activities offer a wonderful way to start mindfulness practice for anyone and especially for active kids who don't like to "sit down and meditate."

Activities for joy, gratitude, and kindness
Connect with your kids and experience joy-boosting and heartwarming activities together. Fantastic for all. Seriously—who doesn't want more joy, gratitude, and kindness in their life?

Activities for emotional intelligence and regulation
Try easy-to-do mindfulness activities designed to offer a simple way to help kids learn about emotions and build emotional intelligence.

Most of the activities can help promote focus, calm, and an improved mood. A focused mind is often a calm mind, and a calm mind is often a happy mind. In other words, you get similar benefits from most of the activities. The reason I divided the activities into themes is to help you with the selection process. For example, if you feel like you could do with a boost of joy and warm feelings of kindness, you might want to pick some of the activities in the category "Activities for joy, gratitude, and kindness." However, if you feel like you want to help your kid focus and feel calmer, you might want to pick some of the activities in the category "Activities for sensory awareness, focus, and calm." And finally, if your child is having a hard time with difficult emotions, or you want to find ways to talk about and experiment with emotions, you might try some of the activities in the category "Activities for emotional intelligence and regulation."

I suggest you get started in the following way... but it's absolutely up to you how you want to proceed:

Browse the activities.

Pick a few that you think both you and the kids would enjoy.

Try the activities yourself before introducing them (alone or with a partner).

Try the activities with the kids when you feel like you've got it.

What Happens Next?

After you've tried a few activities, you might find that...

1. Some activities stick, especially if you both like to do them. Some can even feel as if you might want to do them weekly or daily.
2. Other activities might feel nice to do, but you don't want to practice them daily or even weekly.
3. And some activities just don't feel like your "thing"—and that's perfectly okay.

What you can do next is make a list of the activities you and your kids like and come back to them every now and then.

Like this for example

Activities we might
want to do weekly:

<u>10 sounds</u>

<u>Spot a color</u>

<u>Take five</u>

<u>Beach ball breathing</u>

<u>The Star</u>

<u>Bedtime thank-you's</u>

<u>Gratitude jar</u>

<u>Lovin-kindness</u>

<u>bedtime wishes</u>

<u>Name it to tame it</u>

Activities we might want to do every now and then:

Mindful art

Cooks in the kitchen

Balancing game

Teddy bear breathing

Wish on a star

Sending kind thoughts

What I like about me

Calming glitter jar

Play feelings charades

Read a book with emotion

This is exactly how it works for us at home. We have our go-to activities we do pretty much daily. And then we have other activities we might do once or twice a month. Every now and then, I introduce something new to see how it works out for us— if it sticks. This is how we have built a sustained mindfulness practice at home: with simple, short, and often fun-to-do activities—and with lots of variety.

Eventually... Magic Starts to Happen

When you have sustained your practice for some time, your kids will likely practice some of the activities on their own— especially when they notice that they can benefit from them in a concrete way. Let me share a short story... or four...

Who dares wins

At the time this happened, my son Anton was just two. I woke up at 4:20 to my son crying. He had fallen a few days previously, and his left leg still hurt badly, and his nose was clogged. We offered medicine for pain relief, but he didn't want to take it. Needless to say, it wasn't the best of nights. I wanted to sleep, and for a second, I just hoped that he'd stop crying. That didn't help, obviously, and I gathered all my willpower and decided that I would meditate with him. I wasn't sure it would work, and it felt like a bad idea at 4:21, but I decided to give it a chance.

I walked to the living room with Anton, and he sat in my lap at a window. We watched the dark trees outside, and I guided him to focus his attention on whatever happened outside. A car drove by. The streetlights seemed magical. When he stopped sobbing for a while, I whispered to him slowly, "You know, sometimes our bodies calm down when we pay attention to them." He didn't say anything, and I was afraid he'd start crying again. I felt like I was walking on thin ice.

I took a deep breath and told him that he could put a hand on his belly and that he could actually feel his breath this way. That he might feel his belly go up and down. He nodded and put his hand on his tiny belly. I think he was curious to see if he could feel his breath. I waited a short while and asked him if he could feel his belly move. He nodded again.

We continued to meditate this way, and I asked him if he could feel my belly move against his back as he sat on my lap. He nodded again and laughed a little. I asked him if he'd like to go back to sleep, and he said yes, so we did. The next morning, he explained proudly to Mommy what he had done the night before.

Three-year-old Anton and the super-scary dino

Here's one story that illustrates how mindfulness skills can be used. The cool thing about mindful breathing practice is that... when you practice mindful breathing, you learn to focus and calm down when you most need it. When you want to be calm and cool—instead of overwhelmed and stressed. And when you want to perform better. Have you ever noticed how you do better when you're able to stay focused and calm? I bet you have. Pretty much anything gets easier when you're able to focus, right? My son has discovered this, too!

This happened when Anton was three. He wanted to show his godmother, Carolina, how he could climb this huge playground dino thingy in the park. It was BIG. Huge!

Anton was clearly anxious when he started to climb... and everyone was watching. He starts climbing... he loses his footing a little... and almost falls! Thankfully he doesn't. I was scared, and I'm sure he was, too. Okay, what happens? He stops climbing. Will he quit?

Then he surprises me big time. What he does is he does five mindful breaths... slowly... and all on his own. After the five breaths, he's focused again. He's calm. He has this determined, focused look on his little face. You should have seen his face. He was so cool!

Then he continues to climb... and reaches the top on his own. I was so impressed and proud of him What he did was an activity called "Take five," and then he continued to climb, focused, calm, and confident. He used mindful breathing on the spot to help him succeed when he felt unsure, scared, and overwhelmed. I'm so happy that he knows that he can regain control when life gets tough. Mindfulness is sometimes like a real-life superpower!

Anton guides *me* through practice at age three
We've practiced gratitude for a long time with my son, and he's noticed how it makes the whole family happy. So he started guiding me through gratitude practice when he was three. It started like this. During dinner, I was talking about all the things I felt were wrong. When Anton noticed that I was in a bad mood, he asked me: "Daddy, but what's been *good* today?" He guided me gently to think and talk about the good stuff instead. He joined in, as did my wife. We talked about the good things and even shared a laugh. That changed the mood completely!

My son had helped me change my mood in an instant. With sustained practice, Anton has noticed how he can change the game. This has lead to my son's reminding me to practice when

I'm nervous or stressed, when I make mistakes, and when I eat too fast! Amazing how it goes.

Like just yesterday when he prompted me to take five mindful breaths to improve my badminton game again. That was so funny. Anton saw me fumble with the racket a few times, and he said: "Daddy. Now we meditate!" He had this serious, focused look on his little face. So... we both took five mindful breaths, and we changed the game! We were both able to improve our focus... to pay attention to the game. It's truly amazing to see kids use mindfulness skills to make a real change, to overcome fears, to stay calm, to focus when they want to and to help others. And by the way, pro athletes know this! They do mindfulness to improve their game. Michael Jordan, Kobe Bryant, Shaq, and others meditate to be able to stay present in the game when it matters.

A four-year-old crying and meditating
This happened when we had our winter holiday. We rented a cabin above the Arctic circle in Finland. We had a fun day out playing with reindeer, and we skipped the compulsory nap. At night, we played by the fire and went to bed around midnight. Yikes! This wasn't a normal day for us, and it showed. My wife and I were tired and irritable. Anton was super tired and didn't want to go to bed at all. The situation escalated, and finally he got so angry that he cried. Anton cried and wouldn't do anything we asked him. I wasn't sure what to do and mumbled to my wife something like, "I'm too tired for this." But then, to my amazement, Anton started to meditate in mid cry! I wasn't able to act smart, but my four-year-old was able to self-soothe! He cried and did two breathing exercises (Take five & The star), and he slowly calmed down. I was so amazed that I almost cried too, feeling proud, embarrassed, and happy all at the same time.

As Your Mindfulness Superpowers Grow...

The cool thing is that you become calmer and less irritable when you sustain your practice. You become more aware of your own and your kids' moods and mental states. And you don't become as stressed when your buttons are pushed (because that will continue to happen). When we practice at home, it's easier for us to stay calm when we'd normally get frustrated or even angry. This is pure gold for any parent or educator.

As you become comfortable with mindfulness techniques, you learn to slip them into your routine and even use them on the spot to help your kid deal with difficult situations. When you notice that your kid is getting irritated, you have tools to help them calm down and feel better. You can help your kid do a gratitude, kindness or sensory awareness technique before the situation escalates and irritation turns into overwhelm and upset. Like, for example, when my wife, Hanna, masterfully used a sensory awareness technique to help our son when he was getting increasingly stressed. We were on a much-needed holiday, and Anton was stressed because his godmother, Carolina, was leaving us that day. He was giddy and a little sad, and he couldn't eat or drink at breakfast. He wouldn't sit still, either. To help change Anton's mood, Hanna asked Anton if he could swallow one bite of apple and see if he could feel it go all the way down to his tummy. Anton took one bite and followed the food down his throat. He got excited about it and tried a few more. And he ended up eating his meal.

What Hanna did was she guided him to pay attention to his senses. She knew that paying attention to one's senses has a focusing and calming effect. You will find many activities that do just that in this book, and with some practice, you will be able to help your kid in numerous situations.

Let's Do This!

If you're new to mindfulness with kids, or if you just want to review it, I recommend you read the next chapter headed "FAAQ" and the chapter after that on best practices—it's a short read, and it will help you gain confidence and get started fast. If you feel like you've got this already, then please go ahead and enjoy the activities :-)

CHAPTER 2

FAAQ (FREQUENTLY ASKED AWESOME QUESTIONS)

Is this book for me?

Most likely :-) This book is certainly for you if...

1. You want to kick-start a successful mindfulness practice with kids or teens.
2. You want to find ways to sustain your practice with kids or teens.
3. You want to bring variety to your practice with playful activities.

If you are new to mindfulness, you and your kids can begin the journey together using this book. And if you are already a practitioner, I'm pretty sure you'll find lots of new inspiration. I invite you to try the exercises if you're a parent, grandparent, teacher, therapist or counselor, aunt or uncle. In fact, anyone who wants to connect and build a meaningful relationship with a kid will benefit from this book.

Are you insane—why as many as 150 activities?

I feel fine, thanks for asking. Here's why there's so much to choose from:

1. Kids learn when you do the same core technique in different ways.
2. Different kids prefer different variations of the same technique.
3. Some variations work better for different ages.

The secret sauce in this book is that there's a lot of variety. Variety helps combat boredom, and it helps you find activities that best fit you and your kid. I remember one kid thinking the "Take five" exercise was stupid but "Blowing dandelions" made perfect sense. Essentially, it's the same mindful breathing technique—it's just played out differently. So, for one essential mindfulness core technique, like mindful breathing, you'll find a multitude of ways to practice.

My son has mastered five different ways to do mindful breathing and uses two of them weekly. One activity would be enough to master, but my son thinks it's fun to learn new "games," and the variety helps to keep practice fresh.

You'll find many ways to practice mindful breathing in this book. A younger child might like to do "Hot chocolate" or "Blowing dandelions," and another kid might like to do "Take five" and an older kid "Counting to ten." It's really nice to be able to offer different ways to practice—especially if one activity doesn't feel like a good fit. Similarly, you'll find many ways to practice gratitude. Teens might prefer "Journaling gratitude," and young kids might like to do a bedtime gratitude activity like "Bedtime thank you's."

With this book, you'll never feel that you need to give up mindfulness if your kid doesn't like one activity... there's always something else you can try .

Do you think mindfulness is effective?

Mindfulness is exceptionally effective, in my opinion. You can learn awesome skills to decrease stress and anxiety, pay attention, focus, and calm down. You can learn skills that can help you to notice and understand emotions. You can even learn activities that can help control impulses and nurture compassion and positivity. Numerous studies back this up. But don't take my word for it—try it out for yourself and see how it works for you.

Is my kid old enough to start?

Mindfulness is taught to kindergarteners these days; it's not a big deal. Even pre-schoolers can learn mindfulness skills, and it's beneficial to them. One study showed that a twelve-week mindfulness training (twice a week) helped preschoolers boost mental flexibility, empathy, and academic success, earning higher marks on their end-of-year assessments. You can read more about the study here: www.blissfulkids.com/umab/

We started practicing with our Anton when he was six months, but I haven't heard of many others doing that. Gratitude practice was something we did even back then (Bedtime thank you's). He probably didn't understand what we were saying at first, but the feelings were contagious and clearly soothed him.

We continued with simple sensory activities to build awareness—simply noticing things together. Listening to sounds outside. Inspecting details on leaves. Discovering the world together with curiosity. Gradually we put more effort into recognizing emotions and feelings. Our son learned to notice strong feelings such as anger and frustration. We made fun of them together and explained how everyone experienced them. He began to realize how those emotional states affected him and the people around him. The way my stress would affect him. Parents, too, lose their cool, even parents with a 10-year meditation practice behind them. Big surprise ;-)

Then, just before his second birthday, we began to practice simple breathing exercises together. He learned that his body would calm down when he practiced. Anton came down with the flu and panicked when we had to flush his clogged nostrils. He felt he was drowning. It was the worst. This spurred us to train him in mindful breathing. This rather quick training helped to the point that he agreed to do the flushing. He repeatedly climbed onto my lap and sat down prepared to do it, all on his own with tears in his eyes.

Writing this, remembering it, still makes me emotional. I didn't like it one bit. But he was the brave one! He sat down, and we flushed his left nostril. He cried out, then did his breathing exercise and allowed us to flush the other nostril. Again he cried out, did his breathing, and calmed down in seconds instead of the ten-minute panic attack he had before he learned mindful breathing.

My kid is 15—should I do "12 and up" activities only?

No. The age recommendations are more about how difficult the exercises are than what age they are most suited for. So, for example, 3+ activities work fine for a teen or a grown-up, but 12+ activities are most likely too advanced for children under the age of six. My recommendation is to skim the activities and try the ones that you find interesting and fun. And you might want to start with some of the 3+ activities to introduce mindfulness in a super-easy way, regardless of age.

Should I follow the age recommendations?

No. No kid is the same, and no two 7-year-olds are alike. You know your kid better than anyone else, and you will be able to pick the right techniques for them. The age recommendations are there just to give you a general idea. Please don't let the age recommendations restrict you. I've found out that it's often less about age and more about preferences and sometimes maturity. Many of the activities for "3 and up" work great for teens and grown-ups too. And you might want to start with some of them to introduce mindfulness in a super-easy way regardless of age. These activities can be just as fun and effective for grown-ups as they are for children and teenagers.

Ssshh... now I'll share a secret with you.

Don't tell anyone, okay?

Okay!

Here we go: I'm 40+, and I practice many of the "3 and up" activities myself—daily. You see, those are the ones that are easy to do, and when they are easy to do, then you have a good chance of actually doing them on a daily basis, right? Right! :-)

What if my kid doesn't want to meditate or sit still?

If that happens, then that's perfectly okay! We're all different, and some kids just don't want to sit down and "meditate"—at least not at first. What you can do is introduce mindfulness with sensory awareness activities. Sensory awareness is just a fancy way of saying paying attention to your senses. Try some of those and keep it short. You can even show your kid that you can meditate while eating delicious foods (The raisin meditation & The tasting game). That's an eye-opener.

Many children associate mindfulness with sitting meditation, but mindfulness is much more than that. Sitting practice is just one way to experience and train mindfulness skills. You can introduce mindfulness with fun games like Jenga, Simon Says, a Mindful Walk or the classic egg-and-spoon race (Balancing relay). All are great for developing focusing skills.

You will find many more engaging activities in this book for a high-energy child. Start with active exercises that develop attention skills. After some time of sensory awareness activities with your kid, you might feel okay with some of the other techniques too. Introduce sitting practice later and begin sitting practice with fun sensory awareness activities like "Listening to sounds" and "Sound signal" to make it playful and game-like.

How many activities should I try with my kid?

Try as many as you like, but try not to overwhelm yourself or the kids. Take it easy and introduce one activity at a time, and take some time to see how the kids respond to that particular activity. I would not recommend introducing much more than one per week. And I do hope you don't feel like you need to try out tens of activities – unless you and your kids are having a blast, of course. Learning one or two techniques *well* is enough. The reason there are over 150 activities in this book is just to let you pick from a variety of activities so that you'll find something that sticks and so you can introduce new ones every now and then to keep practice fresh.

What's the difference between adults' and kids' mindfulness practice?

The big difference between adults' and kids' mindfulness activities is that activities for children and youth are usually short and playful. What's really neat about kid's activities is that they work for adults as well and offer a fun way to practice mindfulness together. You learn to focus on demand, self-calm, and speak and listen mindfully, and you grow kinder towards yourself and others.

How often should I practice?

I recommend adults practice every day, even if it's for 30

seconds or a minute. If you don't, it's way too easy to lose the habit.

How often should I practice with my kid/teen?

I try to practice a little every day with my son, even if it's a simple sensory awareness activity like marveling at the moon. Try and see if you can practice twice a week for a start. This is important: it really is enough to practice for just a minute or two. Especially to kids, I recommend that they try a minute or two— a couple of times a week.

Do you practice often?

I meditate daily. I have different practices I do: gratitude practice, loving kindness practice, sensory awareness practices like mindful breathing, and so on. There are days that I meditate for 30 seconds, and then there are days that I meditate for two hours (not that often). Some days I feel like I'm meditating most of the time, when I'm aware and pay attention to my inner and outer life during the day. Some days it's easy to meditate, and other days it feels like there's not enough time... and the funny thing is that it's on those busy days that meditation is most helpful. A few minutes of mindfulness practice can change the way I feel... so that I feel less busy!

How long have you been practicing mindfulness?

In some form or another, for 20+ years. I've been teaching meditation for about 15 years.

Can children learn to do mindfulness activities on their own?

I recommend children begin with an adult. Once children are familiar with the activities, they can practice them on their own, too. The long-term goal should be to help children learn how to use the skills on their own, even on-the-spot when facing difficult situations and emotions—like before a test or a sports performance.

Some children will use techniques they find useful on their own. Still, you shouldn't expect a child to form a habit of mindfulness practice. It's up to you to help them practice. If you're a parent, you're in for a treat. As a parent, you will be able to show your kids how they can apply mindfulness skills when they need it—like doing a few mindful breaths when they get irritated or a round of gratitude practice when they could use a pick-me-up. If you're a teacher you can help the kids practice before a test to reduce test anxiety.

Teens are more inclined to practice on their own, but they need your support too. That is why you need to take care of building your own practice and mindfulness habits first. You will lead the way and make sure you can model it for them. It's like the safety instructions you get on an airplane:

In case of emergency, air masks will drop from the ceiling. If you are traveling with a minor, please put on your own mask before helping the minor.

Should I use mindfulness practice to discipline children?

No. Mindfulness needs to be associated with pleasurable feelings as much as possible, especially in the beginning, so that children look forward to the practice. While a regular practice does promote internal organization and self-awareness, which often leads to better self-discipline, this is an internal process for each individual practitioner and should not be imposed from the outside.

Will I turn my child into a controlled robot?

Aren't children supposed to be impulsive with their thoughts and actions? Isn't that the way of childhood, to live only in the moment and learn the benefits and consequences of those actions? Will teaching mindfulness to my child deprive them of these experiences? These are questions that stem from common misconceptions about mindfulness teaching and children. Mindful awareness doesn't take away the impulsiveness and freedom of childhood. Actually, it encourages creative thinking, problem-solving, and individuality. It is about giving them the tools to be able to choose options other than anger, fear, anxiety, stress, and disconnectedness. Practicing mindfulness allows your child to more freely enjoy the pleasures of childhood.

Can I control my kids with mindfulness?

While having an angelically behaved child can make parenting easier, the goal of mindfulness in children isn't about controlling them and their emotions. Having said that... I must confess that my son sometimes "controls" me. He has learned to gently guide me towards a better mood when I'm down—like a sneaky little mindfulness-ninja!

Why can't I quiet my mind?

The simple answer is, "you don't!" Quieting the mind is not the goal of mindfulness practice in my opinion. The goal is to be increasingly more aware of whatever is happening in a balanced and non-reactive way. Sometimes the mind is quiet, sometimes it isn't. Picture me shrugging here. We run into trouble when we think one is right and the other wrong. Thinking that the goal of mindfulness is to quiet the mind is one of the most common misconceptions people bring to mindfulness—and one of the most common pitfalls of dedicated practitioners! Be aware when you or your child is judging the practice based on such an assumption.

When someone asks me, "How do I keep my mind quiet during practice?" I say, "You don't. You simply notice the thoughts or distractions and then gently refocus on practice."

Is mindfulness scientifically supported?

Yes, in many ways. Some of us (like me) sometimes need scientific evidence to further motivate us, and I made these blog posts (I try to update) for us science nerds.

1. What science says about mindfulness practice with kids, teens, and grown-ups
2. Mindfulness and the brain made easy

You can find the articles here: www.blissfulkids.com/umab/

Is mindfulness religious?

Mindfulness is not a religious practice. Similar techniques can be found in many religious and contemplative traditions globally, but, in our context and when it is used in health care, mental health, and education, it is not.

Could mindfulness be the silver bullet for my problems?

It's not very useful to think of any one practice as the "one thing" that will turn our world around. Steady practice does have a positive impact on people's lives in a relatively short time, but it is not a retreat from the real world and will not prevent challenging external events from happening. What mindfulness often does is create space between events in the world and your response to them. And in that small space, there is great potential for responding to life circumstances in a completely different, healthier way.

How can I explain mindfulness to kids & teens?

To do mindfulness activities, you don't have to explain the concept of mindfulness. It's good to explain, but sometimes you can show instead. Younger kids, especially, want to try it and see for themselves. And when kids have tried mindfulness activities a few times, they will likely get it. They may experience good feelings during and after practice. Perhaps they will feel more focused and less anxious. Maybe they'll experience pleasant feelings of joy, contentment, calm, and kindness. Here are some examples of how you can talk about mindfulness to inspire kids and teens.

To younger kids

You could simply say that:

Mindfulness is…

…noticing what is happening right now.

Mindfulness is taking notice of what you see, hear, smell, touch, and taste. You are being mindful when you smell a flower or listen to the rain. When you pay attention to the wonderful smell of a rose, your mind is focused and calm. You are not thinking about worries. It's as simple as that!

Mindfulness is also paying attention to how your body feels. You can even feel emotions in your body when you pause and notice, perhaps through a tightness somewhere when you're upset, or a good sensation when you're happy. You're being mindful when you notice that you're feeling angry or when you notice that you're feeling excited.

Mindfulness is noticing what your mind is doing, too. Are you daydreaming? Thinking about what happened at school yesterday? Or planning what you'll do tomorrow? You're also being mindful when you notice that you're thinking—maybe you are thinking about a friend or the test at school next week.

You could add that:

Mindfulness is…
…noticing what is happening right now, inside of you and outside of you.

You can pay attention to your thoughts, your emotions, and your senses. And when you do, you are being mindful. You could stop the explanation here and keep it simple, and when you want to expand, you can add two more key qualities of mindfulness: curiosity and kindness. Like this:

Mindfulness is…
…noticing what is happening right now,
inside of you and outside of you,
with curiosity and kindness.

Curiosity is a childlike quality of wonder and awe that powers mindfulness. Curiosity helps us explore, dig deeper, and find new perspectives. It's about smelling that rose and inspecting that spider web. It's about looking at something mundane with new eyes. And it's key for learning, too. When we're curious, we are often less restricted in our thinking and more open to new possibilities.

The kindness part means that we simply notice what's happening without instantly deciding that it's good or bad. We simply notice without starting an internal dialogue about the pros and cons. We are kind to ourselves and others in that way—without judging instantly.

So, to sum it up. When we're mindful, we are aware of what we are doing and experiencing. We observe our emotions, our thoughts, and our surroundings in an even-minded, curious, and nonjudgmental way. We are less swayed by our emotions. We are less reactive, and we can respond from a place of clarity, kindness, and calm. Pretty nifty!

To become mindful more often, we can do playful mindfulness activities. These activities can help you improve concentration, be less anxious, feel more joy daily, and be kinder to yourself and others. Even when you're upset!

To older kids and teens

Teens often want to know more up front. The simplest way to explain mindfulness is to tell them how a specific activity *makes you feel* and *why you want to practice it* yourself. You could also explain how mindfulness often happens on its own—how it's a normal part of life. I'm sure you have experienced many mindful moments spontaneously. Maybe you were paying attention to something closely. Perhaps you were giving your full attention to a loved one, listening to the rain in bed, focusing fully during sports or enjoying a meal with all your senses. Maybe you were enjoying your favorite song or were engaged with your pet. Maybe you experienced adversity and you were able to handle it with a clear and calm mind.

I practice mindfulness to experience more of these balanced and joyful states of mind—to live more skillfully. It helps me be more balanced, more focused, less stressed, and less angry, and it helps me feel content and good about myself. I practice loving kindness activities (for example) so that I judge myself less and can feel better about myself.

You could also simply expand on the previous explanation (for younger kids) and say that mindfulness is a basic life skill that can benefit them in many ways. I like to say that mindfulness activities are like a set of tools that you can use to get different results—like with a Swiss army knife.

You can practice mindfulness to
de-stress and calm down,
navigate difficult emotions,
control impulses and stay cool,
improve focusing skills to perform better,
nurture empathy and self-kindness,
and build more joy, positivity, and happiness.

You can, for example, train yourself to feel more joy and contentment with a simple gratitude activity. Training yourself to feel joy helps you to add many more moments of joy to your days. Who doesn't want that?

You can train yourself in kindness and empathy with a loving kindness activity. It can help you be kinder towards yourself, reduce self-criticism, and bring you more good feelings. It can help you be a better, more compassionate friend, too.

You can learn how to focus on whatever you want to focus on instead of the constant worries our minds tend to focus on. Like when you want to be better at something—when you want to excel at football or improve your guitar skills. To succeed, you want to be able to focus on that one thing to perform better. Mindfulness activities help with just that.

You can even train yourself to pay attention to thoughts and emotions, which then helps you see them for what they are—so that they can't push you around that much anymore. With practice, you get to choose how you want to respond in situations when your buttons are pushed. You can be cool, instead, and respond in a smart way when someone says or does something you don't like. You can respond in a cleverer way, without getting hurt or hurting the feelings of others.

As you create more emotional balance with mindfulness practice, you are less easily knocked down by your emotions, and in moments when you *are* knocked down, you can bounce back faster.

Finally, I think it's important to note that mindfulness practice isn't only about experiencing good feelings. At its core, it's about developing a capacity to live with the full spectrum of human experience—the good and the difficult.

How can I explain why mindfulness works?

Here are some examples of how you can talk about the mechanics of mindfulness.

Calm

You can learn to calm your busy mind when you're anxious, when you do a test or when you need to talk in front of the class at school. How does it work? When you focus on your breath, for example, your busy mind gets a rest—you get a rest from invasive thoughts. When you focus on your senses like that, your mind gets a chance to calm down. This happens because you pay attention to your senses instead of thoughts and worries. My four-year-old son knows this, and he sometimes guides me to pay attention to a flower or to listen to sounds of water to help me calm down and feel better.

Focus

When you practice paying attention to your senses, you improve your concentration skills, too. And you are able to focus on what you want, and this helps you achieve at higher levels in sports, school, or music. It can help you score higher on tests, too. We do better when we're able to pay attention to what we're doing, right?

Emotional regulation

Mindfulness practice helps people deal with difficult emotions.

When you practice mindfulness, for example mindful breathing, you begin to notice how thoughts and emotions come and go— and you become less swayed by them. Being aware of emotions and thoughts is liberating. You see them for what they are, you understand that they will pass, and you get to decide how to respond.

Happiness
Mindfulness practice can even help you feel more joy and contentment. When you spend some time thinking of what you're grateful for or thinking kind thoughts, you often end up feeling calmer and happier. How great is that!

Boosting your brain
Also, according to studies, mindfulness changes your brain. This is something I'm super excited about. Mindfulness helps our brains to do a better job so that you can better deal with difficult emotions and thoughts and ultimately make better decisions. Parts of your brain that manage your response to emotions and thoughts become stronger. And the part that gets aroused reacting to emotions—the amygdala—becomes less active. When we're mindful, we get to decide how we respond to life's challenges and we can make good choices more easily.

How can I explain how mindfulness training works?

You could say that you can train yourself in mindfulness in two ways. The first one is *by training without distractions,* like when you shoot hoops on an empty court to improve your basketball skills. You train in that one thing so that it will be easier for you to succeed when you're in a more stressful situation like a tournament.

The other way to train yourself in mindfulness is *by doing a short exercise on demand* at the exact time when you feel like you need focus, calm or positive feelings, like during a test or just before stepping out on the court at a basketball tournament. This way, you can learn to do a short mindfulness exercise when you want to improve your game or mood—when you're stressed or upset. But to be able to focus and feel better on demand, you first need to practice without distractions. In other words, you want to do the first type of mindfulness practice to support the second, the same way basketball pro's shoot thousands of hoops alone on the court without distractions to improve their game. When you shoot those hoops (or train yourself in mindfulness skills) without distractions, you'll be better able to perform when the weight of the game is on you. And what's really cool is that sustained practice helps you be more focused, calmer, and more positive during the day, even without actively trying to be. Scientists have found that sustained practice actually changes the brain in a positive way.

CHAPTER 3

21 BEST PRACTICES FOR A QUICK START AND A SUSTAINED PRACTICE

You can skip this chapter if you've practiced mindfulness with kids for some time and feel like you've got it. Then again, by reading it, you might pick up something new, too. Maybe you can skim the headings to get started. You decide :-)

1. Let kids be kids

It's important to allow children to be noisy, squirmy, and messy. It really is okay. Support play and laughter. Stillness will come.

2. Whatever happens is okay

Seriously. If your kid gets frustrated and can't focus—then that's okay. If you manage to do 20 seconds, that's okay too. If your child is having trouble with a particular exercise, let him know that it is normal to experience those difficulties sometimes. Or if he is just having trouble focusing or is becoming bored, let him know that those feelings are acceptable and that recognizing them is an important discovery—in fact, one of the goals of mindfulness. Recognizing one's feelings is being mindful! Congratulate him!

Tell him that he is being mindful when he notices, then be curious about his experience and ask him what it is he feels. Is he perhaps bored, or frustrated, or is something competing for his attention? Let him focus on that for a while. This is exactly what it is like to be mindful.

Paying attention to his inner life like this will develop emotional intelligence. Mindfulness isn't about the absence of emotions and thoughts; it's about noticing them so that we can act in more skillful ways instead of reacting automatically when our buttons are pushed. It's about recognizing emotions for what they are and having the option of choosing how to act. Show him that you, too, experience difficulty—be open about it, and share the successes and frustrations with each other.

3. Model it

You can show how you practice and tell the kids how it makes you feel. Simply do the practice out loud so that the kids hear what you do. Then share how the practice makes you feel. Or guide your partner through the exercise so that your kid sees how it works. And again, you can share how the practice makes you feel. When your kid sees how the practice benefits you, they will most likely want to try it out, too, at some point.

4. Practice it yourself & teach what you know

Try out the activities on your own, and when you own it, try the activity with your kids. Depending on the kid, you can guide them, practice right alongside them, ask them to practice alone, or invite them to practice with you.

5. Practice together when you are calm

The best way to introduce mindfulness is by practicing in the moments when you're reasonably calm—both of you, you and your kid.

6. Practice in an environment without distractions

A quiet room, for example. Turn the TV off. Leave your cell phone in another room. Put it on silent mode. Delete the Facebook app and your email app, too... No, wait – that would be awesome but not needed ;-)

7. Keep it lighthearted

If you're relaxed and happy, your children will associate mindfulness with good, connected feelings that they will remember their whole lives. Don't make practice a burden, and never force practice. If you have fun and enjoy it, practice will soon become a habit.

8. Keep practice short

Short practice times are good for kids and help you to keep up the practice. I recommend starting with a just a couple of minutes per session.

9. Start light

Start with a few sessions per week. Guide your child to practice a few times a week. Even a few minutes a week can make a great impact on the whole family. In the long run, I recommend you try to do a little every day to keep the practice going.

10. Don't worry too much about practice

Don't worry when you forget to practice, because it will happen.

11. Feel good about yourself when you practice

Yay, you! Seriously, you are giving your kid and yourself a beautiful gift. If you want to self-reinforce mindful behavior, you can cultivate a sense of success when you do manage to practice.

Be proud of yourself when you remember to practice, and

celebrate after your practice. You can do a fist pump and say "yay" out aloud, or do something else (less goofy) that gives you a sense of accomplishment and victory. This little ritual teaches your brain to want to repeat the practice. This is a fake-it-till-you-make-it thing, but it works.

The same goes for when you practice with your child. Remember to compliment him, whatever happens during practice. Try to find a positive vibe to your practice, and your child will love it.

Small victories keep morale high. Whether you do a fist pump or not, it's a great idea to congratulate yourself for taking time to nourish yourself and your child.

The fact that you are reading this book right now and planning to practice with your kids is reason enough to celebrate. Yay, you! Picture me doing a goofy fist pump here :-)

12. Manage your expectations

Mindfulness should not be made into a big deal, especially in the beginning when the concepts are new. Try not to make practice feel like there's something your child needs to achieve. When children feel like they have to achieve something, practice can quickly become a dreaded chore. I know how easy it is to get excited about all the potential benefits of mindfulness, but you don't want to make it a burden for your child. You probably shouldn't set any other goals than to simply practice together every now and then and make it enjoyable.

13. Don't use mindfulness as a punishment

Mindfulness practice should never be used as a punishment or a response to your own frustrations. If your child is in the midst of a tantrum or some sort of emotional turmoil, the best response is not to order them to go their quiet place and practice mindfulness for ten minutes, like a time-out.

14. Know when to practice

Find the right times to practice. Introduce mindfulness by practicing it in the moments when your kid is calm. Don't make them do it when they are overwhelmed. In fact, don't force anything. Positive experiences and emotions during practice will help children remember and then later apply the techniques on their own.

Later, when you've had the chance to practice plenty and your child is accustomed to a technique, you can help them by reminding them to try out a technique like mindful breathing at the first signs of unease, before they are overwhelmed.

Every habit has to start somewhere, and that place is almost always as a part of a regular routine. Decide on a time or situation in which to begin mindfulness practice. This can be at a time of day when you know you will have a little extra time to devote or during a time of the day when you know your child experiences the most stress, anxiety or difficulty transitioning. For example, some practice at the beginning or end of the school day can make a tremendous difference in an adolescent, especially when done on a regular basis, while taking some time to practice with your child each night before bed can be just what a tense or hyper younger child needs to get a relaxing, good night's sleep.

When something is routine, it becomes familiar, and when we are stressed, we turn towards what we know. Turning towards mindfulness will eventually become instinctual.

Here are some examples of good times to practice:

- When you have a natural break together.
- On a lazy afternoon when you are kicking back.
- Before or after reading a book together.
- Just before homework time—it might just make it a little easier to focus.
- After a meal.
- At bedtime. Some exercises can even help you fall asleep faster.
- When you are transitioning from one activity to another. For example, to settle the buzz when the kids get home from school. Practice can be a way to decompress and focus on the positive—a nice way to shift away from any school- or work-related worries.
- Before softball practice.
- To wind down after an exhausting game.
- To cheer yourselves up when your teen has the "blahs."
- To take a break from television and social media. I do this myself to wean myself from my inbox-checking habit.

If you're a teacher or work with groups, then you can guide a group through practice, for example, at the end of the day to help them transition, first thing in the morning for focus, and after lunch to calm busy minds.

15. Work on building routines

Don't be afraid to challenge yourself when it comes to developing mindfulness routines. For example, maybe your mornings are hectic, and you cannot imagine trying to fit anything more into those precious minutes that begin your day. If you are feeling this way about mornings, chances are your child is, too. But this can actually be the perfect time to develop a simple mindfulness routine.

If you and your child are able to get out of bed just ten minutes earlier, you can have a few moments of mindfulness to prepare yourselves for the day. It can be as simple as asking your child about her feelings. Perhaps she feels stressed or anxious. You can let her know that you feel the same way this morning and that you can both relax and feel better by spending a minute thinking about the things you are grateful for.

The same is also true for those times when it seems like everyone is falling apart and the last thing you need is the task of getting your child to practice mindfulness. In these situations, the first couple of times may be a struggle, but with gentle encouragement and consistency, you may find that those hectic times of day begin to ease and everyone is better able to cope with emotions and stresses.

16. Make it an experiment

Try an activity with the kids a few times, perhaps three to five times, to see if you enjoy it together and if you feel the benefits of practice—if it makes you feel good. You can call it an experiment to get them excited about it. See how it makes you feel the first time you try it out and if the experience changes over time.

17. Let kids try on their own

Teens often want to try on their own, and that's okay. They might not like to be watched when they practice, and that's perfectly fine. But how do you know your kid is ready to practice solo? You can ask questions. Try some of the following questions after you've trained together.

- How did it make you feel?
- Did it make you feel good?
- Did it make you feel a little more focused?

- Did it make you feel a little calmer?
- When would you like to be able to focus like this?
- When would you like to feel a bit calmer like this?
- When do you think this could help you out?
- Would you like to try it on your own sometime?
- Would you like to do an experiment and see if this exercise can help you out sometime?

18. Explain the benefits

Explain how mindfulness can help with stress and anxiety, improve attention and performance, improve self-regulation, nurture positivity, compassion, and kindness. How just a few minutes per day can improve your mood and possibly even the whole day. You will find ideas on how to explain these based on your own experiences when you practice yourself.

To youth you could add that you think it's worth spending two to five minutes in practice so that the rest (1440 minutes) can become much more enjoyable. So that they can pick themselves up when feeling down or focus at will to perform better when they want to succeed.

Help them picture a viable end result, how mindfulness skills could assist them to make positive changes in their lives. What could those be? Be careful not to overpromise, but make them curious about the possible benefits. Maybe there's some area in their life that they could improve with mindfulness skills (academia, sports, arts, hobbies, friendships). Would they be willing to invest a few minutes in order to set themselves up for improved focus, less stress, and a more positive outlook on life?

Finally, tell them how mindfulness has benefited you or someone else they look up to. Ask them if they'd like to see if it works for them, too. To keep it real, it's smart to talk about your own experiences instead of anecdotes and studies only.

19. Make it real for them

Kids are practical. Theory goes only so far. Mindfulness training is beneficial and often makes your child feel both calm and good inside. Yet, the real aha moment happens when your kid experiences the benefits of mindfulness when and where they truly need it—when the training wheels come off. It's about giving them that context to say, "I learned this on the sofa at home, but wow, this really works for me when I'm stressed doing a math test."

If you want your kids to retain the skills, they will have to learn to apply mindfulness in different situations. When your child experiences firsthand that a technique actually helps him in a tough situation, he will likely choose to practice and use it again.

My son has used mindfulness techniques on the spot to overcome anxiety, deal with pain, calm down when nervous, overcome fear, focus on a difficult task to perform better, feel better when mommy was away, and fall asleep when it was tough to do.

The idea is that you learn a few techniques well together and then you show your child how the techniques work for them in real-life situations. The same way when I told my son how he could conquer his fear of the big, yellow, children's slide. Anton already knew the mindful breathing technique, and I helped him realize that he could apply it in a new situation. Later he was able to use the same technique to conquer his fear of climbing the huge dino climber thingy in the park—all by himself. Anton has noticed first-hand how mindful breathing helps him overcome fears and helps him focus. And, from the age of three, he's been able to apply mindfulness techniques on the spot to perform better. It's astonishing!

There's no better way to demonstrate mindfulness than to let kids see how it affects them. This is how you can do it:

a. Give them examples of when activities could be helpful on the spot. Here are some ideas:
    - A few mindful breaths before a test to help with test anxiety.
    - A minute of gratitude practice when feeling bored or upset.
    - A few mindful breaths when they want to focus and perform better during sports or piano practice.
b. Pick an activity that is important for your child, like football practice, a dance recital, a musical performance or a test at school. In some cases, you might be able to be there to guide them through a quick mindfulness exercise, but if you can't, you can, instead, role-play the situation a few times so that they feel confident to try it out on their own. Check the "Mindful testing" activity to see how you can train for an important test at school to reduce test anxiety.
c. Take cues from your kid and help him or her to use mindfulness on the spot by reminding them to try out a technique like mindful breathing or gratitude practice at the first signs of unease.

Mindfulness is a learning journey, one that will take time to grow on you and your kid. You will want to present many opportunities for practice to give your child the chance to experience, understand, and be able to apply the techniques they are learning. But remember to be gentle, and don't expect children to apply mindfulness skills in difficult situations without plenty of prior practice, where they have the opportunity to learn when in a calm and relaxed state.

20. Note how practice is affecting your kid

Remember to look for how practice is affecting your kid—do

they seem to be more settled, happier, more at ease with their life? You know your kid better than anyone else, and you will be able to notice which techniques are helpful.

What we measure we can improve, and when we notice positive change, we will be motivated to continue on our path. So be sure to look for how mindfulness practice is affecting your child. There are four main ways that you will know how mindfulness practice is affecting your child.

1. The first is by your observations—does he or she seem to be more settled, happier, more at ease with his or her life?

2. The second is by asking the child how they feel before, during, and after practicing mindfulness techniques.

3. The third is by asking your child if they would like to continue practicing a specific technique.

4. And the fourth is by asking if they have tried practicing something on their own. You might be surprised. Children can be quick to adopt a practice on their own when they notice the benefits.

21. Hone your own mindfulness superpowers!

This one seems rather obvious. But it's super-duper important to remember to do your own personal practice, too. Practice is like doing push-ups for the mind, and repetition is the key to sustained mindfulness. Repetitive practice helps us to train our brains to become calmer and more aware, even when we are not doing a mindfulness exercise. It is through this practice that we train our minds in how we want them to respond in high-pressure, emotional situations.

Eventually, what we do during mindfulness practice will be more readily available to us when we need help on the spot. It's just like training a mindfulness muscle! If you skip your training, it will grow small. If you keep training, it will be strong when you need it.

Your daily practice session is the foundation of your mindfulness. As you continue this habit, your overall level of mindfulness, and the skilfulness with which you live your life, will continue to increase even at times during the day that you are not consciously practicing. This will reflect positively on your child and environment. WIN WIN WIN!

Urgent Plea!

Are you enjoying this book?

If you like this book, then please help us share it :-)

Please help us share the good,
and write a short review of this book online.

You can do this on the Amazon.com page for this book.

Use this link: www.blissfulkids.com/rate-book/

Or simply do a search for this book on Amazon.com to get started.

It will only take a moment, and it will help this book be found by others too.

CHAPTER 4

ACTIVITIES FOR SENSORY AWARENESS, FOCUS, AND CALM

Sensory awareness activities can help kids

- learn focusing skills,
- increase awareness, reduce anxiety,
- calm down,
- and figure out that paying attention to their senses helps them regulate their emotions.

Sensory awareness is just a fancy way of saying paying attention to one's senses. Paying attention to your senses is probably the easiest way to practice mindfulness. We can pay attention to what we smell, taste, touch, hear or see. Whenever we bring awareness to what we are experiencing with our senses, we are being mindful. When you tune in to your senses, you are effectively living in the now. Your senses are as "in the now" as it gets.

Training yourself to pay attention to your body and your senses can help you to feel less stressed and anxious, calmer, and more focused. When you practice paying attention to your senses, you improve your concentration skills, and you are able to focus on what you want.

I've both practiced and taught mindfulness for years, but I'm still amazed at how the simple act of paying attention to my senses has such a strong calming effect.

Why does this happen? The short answer: when you pay attention to your senses, you shift your focus away from your emotions and thoughts. Instead of worrying about the future or the past, you focus your mind and reduce the brain chatter. It's simple and very powerful.

It's hard to be frustrated and anxious when you are completely focused on your senses because you are fully engaged in the now instead of stuck worrying about the future or caught in regrets. You give your busy brain a much-needed break.

Even a short break from mental chatter can help you to calm down. This is why mindfulness can be so liberating. When you understand this, you can help your child calm down in various playful ways.

We do sensory awareness activities almost daily in some form or another. We listen to different sounds outdoors and indoors. I often guide my son to play these "sensory games" before he gets frustrated. For example, when he sits on the toilet when we prepare to go to bed. And my son reminds me to practice when I'm nervous, stressed, drop the ball or eat too fast!

My son Anton loves to play sensory games. He likes to play "Spot a color" and "10 sounds" when we're preparing to go to bed. He usually asks me to play with him when he is sitting on the toilet after we've brushed his teeth. But to be honest, sometimes I feel like: "Noooooo, the color game again!!! I want to go and read my book already..." but then I suck it up because I know how beneficial it is. The results are always worth the small effort.

Playing these simple games helps my son calm down. Calm is obviously pretty neat at bedtime. As a big bonus, sensory games calm *me* down, as well. I feel less anxious when I play a sensory game, and my mental state is reflected by my son.

And truthfully, I enjoy the game as soon as we start playing. Focusing on my senses, even just for a minute or two, gives me a break from to-do lists, worries, and whatever it is I think I should be doing at that moment. This is awesome at bedtime since I'm often a little anxious to get my son to sleep so that I can finally go do my grown-up things. I wonder if anyone else has ever felt like that? ;-) Anyways... When we play, we're both calmer, and there's less fuss—and I get to go read my book sooner, too.

Let me share a short story called Listening To Raisins:

This is a good story since it shows the use of all senses. Last summer, we had a fun workshop with a group of parents and educators where we listened to raisins together. Yes, you read it correctly... We *listened* to raisins.

Imagine eight grown-ups sitting around a conference table listening to raisins. Yes, it's pretty funny. And I get paid to do that!

Okay, we were doing a popular mindfulness meditation (The Raisin Meditation) where we used all our senses to experience food. After picking a raisin, we took a few slow breaths and focused with each of the five senses:

Sight
What color is the raisin? Is it translucent? Does it have ridges?

Touch
Does it feel bumpy? Soft? How about those ridges?

Smell
Does the smell remind you of anything? How is it different from other foods? Does it smell sweet?

Sound
Can you hear sounds when you bring the raisin close to your ear and squish it gently?

Taste
Can you taste flavors while holding the raisin on your tongue? How about when you bite into it? Are there any flavors left lingering in your mouth after you swallow?

Paying attention to senses like this helps us to focus, slow down, feel a bit calmer, and train our brains to stay present-minded. I'm sure you can appreciate these effects if you have kids. But how did the raisin meditation work out for the parents and educators? Really well! All of them were able to get fully immersed. And yes, all of them could hear sounds when they squished a raisin. I know you want to try it out—and I encourage you to listen to a raisin today!

During that day, the parents and educators learned that they could calm their minds by simply focusing on their senses, it could be that easy to take a break from all the busyness and worries occupying their minds, and all it took to gain calm and clarity was to pay attention to their senses. Then I shared a secret that blew their minds... Are you ready?

Here it is: You can, in fact, do the raisin meditation with a piece of chocolate, too :-) Yes, you can actually meditate and eat chocolate. WIN WIN! And you can do it with your favorite beverage, too.

The good people attending the workshop learned firsthand to meditate with food... and they liked it a lot. And I brought chocolate with me to the next workshop.

Now, go on and try some! The following activities offer a wonderful way to start mindfulness practice for anyone and especially for active kids who don't like to "sit down and meditate."

WARNING!

BE SURE NOT TO MISS SOME OF THE BEST ACTIVITIES.

Please don't let the age recommendations restrict you.

The age recommendations are more about how difficult the exercises are than what age they are most suited for. So, for example, "3 and up" activities work fine for a teen or a grown-up, but "12 and up" activities are most likely too advanced for children under the age of six. "3 and up" activities are often great for older kids, teens, and even grown-ups. And you might want to start with some of them to introduce mindfulness in a super-easy way regardless of age.

3 and up

Sound hunt

Purpose: Mindfulness of sounds and surroundings, Focus, Calm

Best for: Ages 3+, groups or one-on-one

What you need: Access to outdoors, pen and paper is optional

This activity is easy to do, and a great way for kids to focus on their senses. The idea is to teach kids to expand their awareness to their surroundings. Go for a walk together with your child and pause every now and then to listen mindfully to your surroundings. Ask your child what he can hear? Wind in the trees? Traffic? Footsteps? Bees buzzing? A dog barking? Birds tweeting? Make a note of what you hear.

Face bath
Purpose: Body awareness, Focus, Calm

Best for: Ages 3+

What you need: Nothing

This is a simple activity that teaches your child to pay attention to sensations in his body.

Ask your child to rub his hands together to warm up through friction. After 10 to 20 seconds, tell him to lift his hands to his face. Tell him to move his hands slowly over his face like when drying his face with a towel. Ask him if he can feel the warmth of his hands. How does it feel?

Talk about how it felt. Was it nice? Was it calming to focus on the sensations?

Mindful claps
Purpose: Body awareness, Focus, Calm

Best for: Ages 3+

What you need: Nothing

The idea behind this activity is to pay attention to sensations in your body.

Ask your child to stand or sit with his hands shoulder-width apart. Tell him to clap his hands together two times so that he returns his hands to the original position between each clap.

Next, ask him to close his eyes and pay attention to how it feels to clap now. Tell him to clap three more times and pay attention to what he feels in his hands and fingers.

When done clapping, ask him to be still for a moment and to pay attention to how his body feels. Ask him how his arms, hands and fingers feel. Talk about how it felt clapping and how his body felt afterwards.

Squish and let go

Purpose: Body awareness, Focus, Calm, Relaxation

Best For: Ages 3+, groups or one-on-one

What you need: Comfortable clothes, ample floor space (or another place to lie down)

This is a great exercise to help your child let go of tension and become more mindful of his body. Tell your child that you will see if you can you feel the difference between when his muscles are tensed and when they're relaxed. You can use the following script with your child. You can sit, stand or lie down. If you lie down, you'll need to alter the script a little bit.

Guided script:
Take three deep breaths.

Now we'll start tensing and relaxing each part of the body, starting with the toes.

Toes

Imagine you are an ape in a tree. Apes hold on to branches with their feet. Clench your toes. Curl them like grabbing a branch with them really hard. One. Two. Relax the toes. Let them go limp.

Notice how nice it feels.

Legs
Let's try your legs. Clench your legs. One. Two. And release.

Notice how nice it feels. See if you can you feel the difference between when the muscles are tensed and when they're relaxed.

Stomach
Next, imagine someone throws a basketball at your stomach. So make your stomach hard. Tighten your stomach muscles. One. Two. And release.

Hands
Now, pretend you are squeezing lemons in your hands. Squeeze really hard. One. Two. And release.

Notice how it feels to relax you hands and arms like this.

Good.

Arms
Now stretch your arms high above your head. Feel the pull in your shoulders. One. Two. And let your arms drop down. (If lying down, be careful to lower arms gently). Let your arms dangle at your sides. Like cooked spaghetti noodles. Notice how relaxed they feel.

Head and shoulders
Imagine you are a turtle pulling his head inside his house. Pull your shoulders up to your ears and push your head down. One. Two. And relax.

Notice how good it feels to relax like this.

Face
Now, clench your face. Make a silly face with as many wrinkles as you can. Scrunch your nose. Clench your jaw. One. Two. And relax.

Good.

Take three deep breaths and notice how your body feels now.

Notice if your body feels good and warm. What else can you feel in your body?

When done, ask your child how his body feels. How did it feel to tense up? How did it feel to let go? Now that you have visited each muscle of your body, tensed, and let go, are you more relaxed or more tense?

Yoga and mindful movement

Purpose: Body awareness, Mindful movement, Focus, Calm

Best for: Ages 3+, groups or one-on-one

What you need: Some floor space to move freely

Mindful movement and yoga are relaxing. You can start with something simple like the tree pose.

The tree pose is super simple yet a little challenging as you need to stand on one leg. You need to focus on your body to be able to stay in the pose for a longer time.

You can make yoga playful if you wish. We "play" yoga with my son. We made the tree pose into a story! First, Anton pretended to be a seed all curled up on the floor. Next, he slowly grew to become a tall tree (the full tree pose). Then we pretended that it got windy. He pretended his arms were branches swaying in the wind. In this posture, you can alternate between different poses with your arms. You can hold your hands on your heart, spread them out to the sides or hold them above your head. Also, you can make balancing easier by placing your foot lower on the supporting leg instead of high up on the knee—even on the floor to help young children get started. Finally, we pretended that it was night, and he closed his eyes. We did that to see how it felt to balance his body without the help of eyesight.

You don't have to do all this to do yoga, of course. I just wanted to demonstrate how you can make yoga practice playful if you wish.

Mindful snack break
Purpose: Sensory awareness, Focus, Calm

Best for: Ages 3+, groups or one-on-one

What you need: Snacks

My son loves to do these little picnics. We pack different nuts and dried berries, like goji, raisins, and mulberries in a small plastic bag and go out and play. We take a break sitting on the porch and practice eating mindfully. It's super relaxed and fun...

We pick one thing from the bag, observe it, smell it and taste it slowly. Sometimes we close our eyes and try to discriminate the textures as well as the tastes. Sometimes we see if it tastes different from how it smells. We discuss the difference between the berries and nuts. Sometimes we mix them and to see what kind tastes we can notice and what happens when we combine salty and savory. Sometimes we sit like this for a minute or two, sometimes we just devour the berries like panthers—yes, we growl like panthers occasionally, too.

A mindful mini-picnic is a fun way to connect, and it has become a habit for us. It's like a mini version of the Raisin Meditation that feels completely natural and fun to do.

The mindful drink

Purpose: Sensory awareness, Focus, Calm

Best for: Ages 3+, groups or one-on-one

What you need: Your favourite drink

This is a favorite of mine! I do this myself with a cup of tea almost every day. What you do is you fire up your senses:

You smell the tea / coffee / hot chocolate brewing,

you feel the warm cup,

smell the hot beverage,

pay attention to the color of the drink, the tea leaves and the steam rising from it,

and then you finally taste it,

and notice the feelings of warmth as you swallow the beverage.

It's simple, it's easy, and you can make a habit of it at home and at work to add a few mindful minutes to your day. You can do it with kids too with almost any beverage to slow life down a little bit.

The tasting game

Purpose: Sensory awareness, Focus, Calm

Best for: Ages 3+, groups or one-on-one

What you need: 5 different foods that fit inside a child's palm (apple slices, raisins or other dried fruit, orange segments, lemon segments, cookies, popcorn, grapes in halves for small children, etc.)

This is similar to the Raisin Meditation, but the difference is that you can easily make this into a game for a group of kids. Tell your child this is a tasting game and that the idea is to use her senses to focus on the food and guess what it is. Ask her to try to be silent during the activity and share her experiences only after she's eaten the food.

Ask your child to close her eyes and carefully place a small piece of food in her hand. Ask her to notice how the food feels in her hand—to simply think about it. Is it soft, hard, squishy, wet, dry, smooth or bumpy? Is it cold or warm?

Ask her to lift the food up to her nose and smell it. Does it smell like anything?

Next, ask her to put the food in her mouth, but not to take a bite just yet. How does the food feel? Can she feel a texture? Does the texture feel different when it's in her mouth compared to when she held it in her hand?

Ask her to bite into it. Is it soft or hard? Is it crunchy? Wet or dry? What does it taste like? Is there more than one flavor? Sweet? Sour? Salty? Spicy?

Ask her if she's ready to swallow. Is she able to feel her throat getting ready to swallow?

After she has swallowed, ask if she could feel the food sliding down her throat. And if there are any flavors left lingering in her mouth.

When she's ready, ask her what the food was and when she figured it out. Ask her how it felt to focus like this and if she'd like to continue with another piece of food.

Cooks in the kitchen
Purpose: Sensory awareness, Focus, Calm, Connection

Best for: Children 3+, groups or one-on-one

What you need: A recipe (or part of a recipe) that your child could safely help cook

Food is a phenomenal way to integrate mindfulness into a child's daily life. Every child eats, and many children eat without really thinking about or understanding where their food comes from. Cooking with children can be a simple, fun, and engaging way to introduce them to mindfulness and help them begin to use their senses (particularly smell and taste) to experience the world around them.

Baking may be the easiest form of cooking to do with a child because it generally involves preparation away from a hot stove and without sharp knives, etc., but any recipe will do. If it is age appropriate, have your child help pour, measure, and mix, and explain to him the effect of each of his actions. All children, from the smallest toddler to the biggest teen, can "help" by experiencing the taste and smell of specific ingredients during the cooking process. It's a great idea to have your child smell and taste ingredients before they are combined in a recipe; he will then better understand how the items come together to make a delicious united whole.

This simple act that we devote time to every day can become a soothing routine as your child grows and becomes an adult. Food, its preparation and consumption, is a sensory experience. Help your child see this by encouraging him to feel, smell, and taste the ingredients. Let him see the transformation of the beginning ingredients into the final dish.

Remind him that with attention, focus, and care we can turn these otherwise ordinary ingredients into food that nourishes our bodies and is enjoyable, just as we can turn life situations into nourishing and enjoyable experiences.

Broken telephone

Purpose: Mindful listening, Focus

Best for: Ages 3+, groups

What you need: Nothing

This is a popular game that is perfect for learning how to listen mindfully. The idea is to pass around a message by whispering it to the next person. Explain that the objective is to pass the message exactly like they hear it. Line up the children and whisper a message to the first child. That child will, in turn, whisper it to the next child in line. The message passes like this all the way to the last child in line. The last player announces the message to the whole group. Comparing how the message ended up to how it began is the fun part.

The message often gets altered along the way. Errors accumulate along the line and the end result is often funny when compared to the original message. Ask them why they think the message changes when they pass it through the line. Were they impatient or anxious, or simply so excited that they might have heard and told the message in different ways? Is it hard to listen carefully when you are excited? Or did someone change it on purpose? It's all okay. Ask them if this could be how rumors and gossip form.

Freeze up
Purpose: Mindfulness of sounds, Focus

Best for: Ages 3+, groups or one-on-one

What you need: A selection of upbeat music

Arrange a dance party with your child or a group of children. This is a fun activity to do with a group. Be sure to find music that matches the age of the children. Encourage them to dance to the music as you play a few songs. Join them and have fun. Next, demonstrate the idea to them. Pretend that you are dancing and hum a song. When you suddenly stop humming, you freeze. Show them how you can freeze in funny positions. When you continue humming, you continue to dance again.

Next, ask them to listen to the music and dance freely, then freeze when the music stops. Play music and let them dance. Start and stop the music. Continue dancing when the music continues. Vary the frequency at which you stop and start the music.

After a few songs, ask them if it was easy to notice when the music stopped. Was it fun? I bet it was :-)

Mindful art
Purpose: Sensory awareness, Focus, Calm

Best for: Ages 3+, groups or one-on-one

What you need: Art materials of choice

Creating art is lovely. It can be as simple as drawing in the sand at the beach, fully immersed in the task—like a mandala type of thing. The secret to mindful art is simple. You simply pay attention to what you're doing. You pay attention to your senses.

If you like to make bracelets, then you can feel the different beads with your fingers ... the difference in the textures ... how the wooden ones compare to the plastic beads ... how about the stone beads? Can you feel a difference in temperature, size, and texture? You look at the different colors and shapes. You might even smell them. This immersion in your art is mindfulness. Focusing on your senses is being mindful.

You know, way back when I did oil paintings, I loved the immersion. It felt awesome to move my body and to feel the thick paint and to simply look at the beautiful colors. When I did that, my mind calmed down and I forgot about my worries. And what's cool about art is that you can sometimes spot how you felt when you created the art. See if your art becomes different depending on how you feel. What does your art look like when you're angry or sad? What does your art look like when you're happy? You can express your feelings with art—and be mindful of your feelings that way, too.

Mandala art
Purpose: Sensory awareness, Focus, Calm

Best for: Ages 3+, groups or one-on-one

What you need: A square surface (a piece of cardboard for example)

A selection of safe and natural materials such as shells, stones, beans, macaroni, leaves, acorns, petals etc.

The idea of this activity is to be present and to focus on the here and now. Show your child examples of geometric art made of natural materials. Google the words "shell mandala" or "stone mandala." Coloring books for grown-ups include these beautiful geometric shapes.

Mandalas are used in art therapy and as an aid in meditation in Hinduism and Buddhist traditions. But for this purpose it is just a geometric design—a beautiful pattern. Creating it, paying attention to the process of building it has a focusing and calming effect, like drawing patterns in the sand. Show nice examples and point out shapes, patterns and symmetry. Let your child choose the materials they would like to work with. Provide a surface such as a piece of cardboard and give him five to ten minutes to work on his art. Tell him to simply focus on his art and try to stay silent during the activity. When you do this activity in a group, silence will help them focus (you can play music to help with that).

When your child is done, talk about his artwork and how it felt to do it. When ready, practice sweeping the art away if you wish—this will help your child learn to let go. The art of letting go can help us release unhealthy attachments to cravings and regrets.

Mindful play
Purpose: Recognition of sensory differences, Mindfulness of body, Focus, Calm

Best for ages 3+, groups or one-on-one

What you need: Sensory play items such as finger paint or craft dough

Set up an area for your kid to have some messy, sensory,

creative play. Pick hands-on play materials such as paint, dough, sand, etc. that your child can play with using his hands. Encourage him to play naturally while noticing how the materials feel on his hands and what he is inspired to do from those sensations. If he gets distracted or has an urge to clean his hands, first have him describe his feelings. Maybe the sand is gritty between his fingers and it is making him uncomfortable. Help him notice how smooth water running over his fingers changes his feelings. Or maybe the coolness of finger paints brings to mind something specific that he wants to paint. Help your child to recognize the connection between physical sensations and emotions, thoughts, and actions.

Object observation

Purpose: Sensory development, Connection with surroundings, Focus, Calm

Best for: Ages 3+, one-on-one

What you need: Approximately five small objects of varying weight, size, and texture (e.g., a sponge, a crumpled piece of paper, a rock, a piece of gummy candy, a match)

You can present this activity as a game to a younger child; an older one might be more reflective without the "game" label.

First, ask your child to sit on the floor or at a table, and tell him to close his eyes. He might like to take some deep breaths to settle in before he begins.

Next, ask him to hold out his hands. A bit of trust is necessary here; make sure that prior to starting the activity he knows that nothing "scary" or "yucky" will be handed to him.

When he is comfortable, place one of the objects in his hands. Once he is holding the item, ask him to silently observe its weight, texture, and size. What does it feel like in his palm? What happens if he moves it from hand to hand? Do different parts of the object feel different, or is it the same throughout?

Continue the process for as long as your child is engaged. When it's over, if your child is old enough, have a conversation about his observations. Were there items that made him feel more comfortable or excited than others? Some that made him particularly curious? Why?

Sensory box

Purpose: Sensory development, Tactile sensory awareness, Focus, Calm

Best for: Ages 3+, groups or one-on-one

What you need: A bin or box and items to fill it (based on the child's preferences and age). It can be a mix of items or many of one type.

Here are some examples:

- Cotton balls
- Felt
- Sand
- Marbles
- Dry pasta or rice
- Grass or leaves
- Pudding or shaving cream (if you don't mind a mess)

This is a more elaborate version of the Object Observation exercise. First, determine an appropriate time of day to utilize the sensory box. Perhaps bring it out when your child first wakes up from a nap, for example, to help stimulate his senses; or maybe give him the box at another time when he needs a quiet moment. You can also designate a calm space where he can explore the sensory box if you wish. When you first introduce it, tell your child to put his hands into the box and describe what he feels. Have him pick up different materials or objects and ask him to compare the way they feel in his hands. How does the object feel against the back of his hands? Against his palms? What happens if he uses only his fingertips?

If your child responds positively to this tactile relaxation technique, try creating a few different sensory boxes and alternate between them.You might also want to make a sandbox or sand play table that your child can play with whenever the mood strikes.

Feel the beat

Purpose: Body awareness, Energy awareness, Focus

Best for ages 3+, groups or one-on-one

What you need: Just your body!

This is a great activity for when you have younger children with an abundance of energy. Bring your child to a safe place and first have her close her eyes and place her hands on her chest and abdomen. Teach her how to feel the breath entering and leaving her body, along with the thumping sensation of her heart.

Next, have her engage in some physical activity like running in place or jumping up and down. After one or two minutes, have your child stop and repeat the part of the exercise where she feels her breathing patterns and heartbeat with her hands. Ask her what she is feeling and what changes she can notice. Use this to illustrate how our bodies and minds are affected by physical activity.

Walk on a rainbow

Purpose: Awareness of surroundings and details, Focus, Calm

Best for Ages 4+, groups or one-on-one

What you need: A nice day

This is a simple activity that will teach your child to be mindful of his surroundings. Before you begin, remind your child of the colors of a rainbow (red, orange, yellow, green, blue, indigo, violet).

Then step outside for a walk. Throughout the walk, ask your child to find something to represent each color of the rainbow. He could bring a small notebook to jot down his answers or he could simply take note of them in his mind. Depending on where you are walking, some colors may be more difficult to locate than others; this is part of the fun! Try to keep walking until he's found a representative for every color. As he grows, this strategy might turn into a daily mindfulness habit.

Sound signal
Purpose: Mindfulness of sounds and surroundings, Focus, Calm

Best for: Ages 4+, groups or one-on-one

What you need: A bell, a phone with sounds, a spoon and a glass, chimes, or any other item that makes a lingering sound

The Sound Signal activity helps children to sharpen their focus and calm down. It's fun to do as well. Mindful listening can be very helpful at school and when friends and family need our full attention. This mindfulness activity involves listening to a sound; many children naturally gravitate toward visual information, so this is a great way to help them become more aware of the auditory information that surrounds them.

To begin, ask your child to sit or lie comfortably. Ask her to close her eyes and breathe deeply for three or four breaths.

Next, explain that you're going to make a sound, and that she should try to focus on the sound until she can't hear it anymore. When she can no longer hear the sound, she will give a signal of her choice. For a younger child, this part of the activity can be made especially engaging or fun. When the sound disappears, she can signal by opening her eyes, raising her hand or snapping her fingers or through a different signal of her own invention. Tell your child that she should listen very hard for the sound for as long as she can and only signal when it is completely inaudible.

Repeat the activity as many times as she likes, perhaps changing the "sound's end" signal with each trial.

Ask her questions about how the activity made her feel. Did she hear the sound longer than she expected? What happened to the sound as time progressed?

Listening to sounds
Purpose: Mindfulness of sounds and surroundings, Focus, Calm

Ages 4+, groups or one-on-one

What you need: A timer or clock

For younger children, you may want to approach this exercise as a kind of game; the game approach may be unnecessary for older children/teens.

Sit with your child in a calm, quiet place. Tell her that you're going to set the timer for 20 seconds. During the 20 seconds, ask her to close her eyes and focus only on sounds. At first, she might protest – the room may be quiet. There aren't any sounds to be heard! Try not to give away that in the next 20 seconds, she'll definitely hear sounds: the sound of a plane or car outside, a clock ticking, an appliance humming, the roof creaking, her ears buzzing. See how many different sounds you can "collect." After the initial 20 seconds (you may practice the exercise along with her), ask her what she heard. If she says she didn't hear anything, tell her what you heard, and let her try listening for another 20 seconds.

Older children and teenagers may be able to participate in increments longer than 20 seconds; build up to a session time that is challenging but comfortable for the individual child.

When ready, ask your child what sounds surprised her. Was there any noise she heard that she could not recognize? Ask her if it was challenging. If you're playing with an older kid, you can ask if she noticed thoughts during the game.

A simple version of this exercise can be used to calm down and to find focus "on the spot," when anxious or overwhelmed. To do this, simply listen mindfully for a minute and try to hear at least five different sounds.

Mindful mystery touch
Purpose: Tactile sensory awareness, Creative and critical thought processes, Focus

Best for ages 4+, one-on-one

What you need: Assorted objects with varying textures, shapes, etc.

Gather some random objects that you have around the house or that you have found in nature. Try to have an assortment that includes items that are smooth, rough or fluffy, along with different sizes.

Have your child close her eyes and hold each item in her hand without knowing what it is. Next, ask her to describe the object and the way that it feels in her hands. Make notes of each item for discussion after the exercise, if desired. If you are working with more than one child, replace the items and let the next child describe the items that the first child had.

Once the activity is finished, you can compare the descriptions and use the opportunity to express how we can single out our senses and how what one person notices may be different from what another person notices.

Washing hands mindfully
Purpose: Mindfulness of Body, Focus

Best for: Ages 4+, groups or one-on-one

What you need: Soap, water, and somewhere to wash your hands

Yes, seriously, you can wash your hands mindfully. Just add curiosity! You can do almost anything mindfully. Try washing your hands mindfully for a day and then tell your child to try it. How does washing your hands really feel? Slow down and feel the flow of water. Watch the water flow. Feel the soap. How does it feel in your hands? Feel the cloth you dry your hands with. Take your time and enjoy it! You have just learned to pay attention better.

Guided script:
Pause and pay attention.

Observe and feel the water, smell the soap, enjoy the feel of damp, clean hands.

Really pay attention to what you're doing and how it feels.

Be curious and take your time.

Tell him to try it for the rest of the day, or the next day, without your guidance, and to check back with you after a day of mindful hand washing. When you get together to discuss his experience, ask him how it was. How often did he remember? Was it nice, did it feel soothing? How did it make him feel, and would he like to try to do something else mindfully?

The mindful fist
Purpose: Body awareness, Focus, Calm

Best For: Ages 4+, groups or one-on-one

What you need: Comfortable clothes, ample floor space (or another place to lie down)

This simple and practical activity will help your kid tune in to their senses for a short while. Tuning in to their senses like this can help them focus and calm down. Ask your child to clench his fists really tightly for 10 seconds and to pay attention to how it feels. After ten seconds, ask your child to release his hands and to pay attention to how his hands feel.

This quick exercise helps him to learn focusing skills and to become more aware of his body. You can expand this by trying out the Squish and Let Go activity and Body Scan for Younger Children.

Body scan for younger children
Purpose: Body awareness, Focus, Calm, Relaxation

Best for: Ages 4+, groups or one-on-one

What you need: Comfortable clothes, ample floor space (or any other place to lie down)

This activity asks your child to think about parts of his body that he otherwise probably doesn't notice. Some of the questions may seem silly to little ones, so it's a great idea to model the activity first while thinking aloud.

The first time your child attempts a body scan, ask him to lie down; make sure he's wearing comfortable clothes and the room isn't too hot or too cold.

Start at the top of his head, and tell him to think about how different parts of his body "feel," moving down the body from his head to his toes as the activity progresses. You might ask things like: How does your hair feel? What about your forehead? What's happening with your ears today? Are they feeling like ears? Bring your attention to your shoulders. Think about how they might move a little as you breathe in and out. And so on and so forth all the way to his toes. Some of these questions may elicit giggles from your child; he's probably never thought about what his hair "feels like." Giggles are okay, of course, but this is why it's a fantastic idea to provide a model of your own before asking him to participate. As you think aloud, use relatable words. For example, you might say, "My hair feels soft and twisty," or "Today my forehead is a little tingly in the middle." When it's over, ask your child how it felt and how he feels now.

When I first started with my son, I used to touch the body parts gently to help him focus on them. I caressed the top of his head and asked how it felt, and so on. You can also start with the "Squish and let go" exercise to get used to body sensations.

Smell and tell

Purpose: Sensory awareness, Focus, Calm

Best for ages 4+, groups or one-on-one

What you need: Items with varying scents

Here are some examples:

- Coffee beans
- Tea
- Mandarin peel
- Cocoa
- Cardamom
- Fresh cilantro
- Apple slices
- Banana slices
- Raisins
- Ketchup
- Mustard
- Peanut butter
- Popcorn
- Spices
- Essential oils
- Vanilla
- Cinnamon
- Almond oil
- Grapefruit oil
- Peppermint
- Lavender
- Pine needles
- Scented soaps
- Scented candles

Smell is a powerful emotional tool and can be an incredible calming and centering aid for mindfulness.

Choose several items with different scents. I recommend a minimum of five. Even with five scents, the game was too short for my son. If possible, keep the scents as natural as possible. If you use edible foods for the scents, then you can end the activity with a snack. Yum! Think about using things such as a freshly bloomed flower, fresh or dried herbs, citrus peels, grass, etc.

Fill small containers with the items. Muffin liners are great! Old cleaned spice containers, baby food jars, and paper cups work well too. I recommend that you cut five little paper cups in half and put a little food or whatever you choose in each. If you're using something wet like essential oils for the scents, then go with plastic cups or glass.

Have your child close his eyes and inhale the scent carefully while focusing only on what he is smelling. Do not encourage him to touch the item, as that may distract his sensory experience. Talk about what he smells and how that smell makes him feel or what it reminds him of. Talk about the differences in the scents. Is something sweet? Does it smell fresh or yucky?

Mindful walk aka spot three things
Purpose: Sensory awareness, Focus, Calm

Best for: Ages 4+, groups or one-on-one

What is needed: A place to walk freely outdoors (a park would be perfect)

My favorite awareness-building, calming exercise is to take a walk in nature. A park will do fine. I start with relaxing my eyes and just noticing what is happening around me. The bird in the tree that I did not notice seconds earlier. The leaves fluttering in the wind. The grass moving as the wind brushes over it. Bees busy in the flowers.

Next, I listen to what is happening around me and try to distinguish between at least five different sounds. A dog barking. The wind in the leaves. The buzz of the bees. Someone laughing. The hum of traffic far off. A bird flying and so on.

Then, I try to feel kinesthetically. I can feel the wind brushing the hairs on my legs. I can feel the sun warming my face. Tall grass brushing past my ankles.

Finally, engaging my sense of smell, I distinguish specific flowers. The grass has been cut this morning. I can even smell the effect of sun on my skin.

Mindfulness practice is not complicated, nor does it take long to do, yet it has the power to bring serenity and bursts of happiness to an otherwise hectic day.

With kids, you can simply go out for a walk together. You ask the kids to spot different things. You can, for example, ask them to notice three different sounds. Give them a few minutes and ask what they heard. Perhaps they heard birds and crickets, or maybe a car that drove by?

After that, you can ask them to notice three things they smell. Again, give them enough time to explore and then ask them what they found. Maybe they smelled freshly cut grass, a hot dog vendor, and flowers?

If you're in a park, you could ask them to notice three animals next. Or three different shades of green. You can do endless variations of this. It's a fun and relaxing activity. Also, you can either walk together, or you can send the kids on missions and wait for them to report back.

The raisin meditation
Purpose: Sensory Awareness, Focus, Calm

Best for: Ages 4+, groups or one-on-one

What you need: One raisin (or other dried fruit) per child

The raisin meditation is a great way to practice mindfulness through the process of eating. You will need to verbally guide your child through this meditation. At first, it's probably a good idea to model the process yourself to show the child exactly what to do; you can "think aloud" when you model the process, but when it's the child's turn, she won't need to narrate in the same way.

To begin, ask your child to pick up her raisin and look at it. Ask her to imagine that this is the first time she has ever seen something like it. Ask her to silently observe its size, color, and texture.

Next, ask her to feel the raisin between her fingers. Does it have bumps and ridges? What does the weight of the raisin feel like in her palm?

Have her bring the raisin to her nose. Does its smell remind her of anything? How does it smell different from other foods? Does this make her want to eat it?

Ask her to bring the raisin close to her ear and to squish the raisin gently. Is there a sound to be heard?

Ask her to bring the raisin to her lips, but not to put it in to her mouth yet. How does it feel? Does she feel an urge to eat it?

Next, ask her to put the raisin on her tongue... but tell her not to take a bite just yet! Does the texture feel different when it's in her mouth compared to when she held it in her hand?

After she bites into the raisin, ask her to think about its flavor. Is there more than one flavor? Sweet? Sour? Salty? Spicy? How does the raisin feel in her mouth now? Is it soft or hard? Is it crunchy? Wet or dry?

Finally, once she has swallowed the raisin, ask her to determine what flavors are left lingering in her mouth.

To wrap up the exercise, ask the child what she learned from eating slowly and mindfully. Was it different to the way she's used to eating? Could focusing attention like this help her in other activities?

Mindful eating
Purpose: Sensory awareness, Gratitude, Connection

Best for: Ages 4+, groups or one-on-one

What you need: A meal

Once a month, or more often if it feels right, have a mindful family meal. Set the table for this special occasion intentionally. Bring the food to the table and then be in the moment. Smell the food before you serve it. Look at the colors on your plate. Take one small bite and really pay attention to how the food tastes, how it feels on your tongue, how it feels to swallow. Continue intentionally with each bite, each smell, each color, each flavor, being fully aware of your meal.

When the meal is over, go around the table and thank one person or animal who helped get this food to you. Thank the person who put the red bell peppers on the shelf at the grocery store. Thank the truck driver who delivered the food to your area. Thank the factory workers who helped assemble your stove. Thank the workers who helped make the paper labels on the cans you used. It's amazing how many "thank you's" there are to be given as you consider the community that fed you this meal.

This activity will help your child recognize that it takes many parts to make a whole, or in other words, everything that we do is connected to somebody else and our energy, thoughts, and deeds affect people and situations that we cannot yet see.

Am I a lefty or a righty?

Purpose: Body awareness, Focus

Best for: Ages 4+, groups or one-on-one

What you need: A meal

Ask your child to eat a meal using her non-dominant hand. Best if you decide to do it together. Here's how to do it:

Place your fork in the hand that you don't use for writing. Now, eat your entire meal this way. Is it difficult to stab or scoop the food? Are you a bit awkward at getting the food into your mouth? Does it take much longer to eat a meal this way than with your dominant hand? How might people who have physical disabilities feel when they have to eat a meal awkwardly? Do they really need to pay attention to what they are doing in order to get the food from the plate to their mouth? Do you need to pay close attention now while you are using your other hand?

Take your time, enjoy the experience, and reflect.

Walking mindfully

Purpose: Body awareness, Mindful movement, Focus

Best for ages 4+, groups or one-on-one

What is needed: Your body and a place to walk freely

This is an excellent exercise when you are ready to get a little fresh air or work off a little energy yourself. Walking Mindfully is simply going for a walk and noticing the different sensations your body feels as you move along. Things you may want to point out and focus on include the rate at which you are breathing, the feeling of breathing while moving compared to when you are still, how your arms move as you walk, what different surfaces feel like under your shoes as you move your feet, etc.

The point is to not overwhelm your child with all of the different sensations but notice them one at a time. For example, after noticing the movement of his arms, add in the feeling of warm or cool air against them as he moves. This way he will gradually realize how he can notice more than one thing at a time and how different aspects work together to produce new sensations.

Mindful standing

Purpose: Body awareness, Mindful movement, Focus

Best for: Ages 4+, groups or one-on-one

What you need: Somewhere to sit

We stand up and sit down tens of times a day. We can do this simple activity mindfully if we wish, to bring us back to the present moment. We can do this by standing up, and sitting down very slowly and paying attention to our whole body as we do it. It's probably a good idea to demonstrate this activity first by doing it yourself. You can explain what you feel in your body as you do this.

To begin, ask you child to sit down. Sit still for about twenty seconds and ask him to pay attention to how his body feels.

Then, ask him to try to be as slow as possible. Like a snail. If you do this with a group you can make a game of it and see who is the slowest.

Ask him to stand up super slowly and to pay attention to his body all the way.

When he is finally standing, ask him to sit down super slowly and to notice what he feels in his body as he does it.

When ready ask him what he noticed and how it felt to do something really slow.

Beanbag balancing game

Purpose: Body awareness, Focus

Best for: Ages 4+, groups or one-on-one

What you need: A beanbag (per player)

This is a simple game. The idea is to give your child a beanbag and have him balance it on his head. To make the game fun, ask him to walk and balance the beanbag on his head. Ask him to walk slowly and fast, backwards and sideways. To take it to the next level, ask him to dance to music while balancing the beanbag on his head. The game requires both focus and body awareness and is a lot of fun with a group of kids.

Simon says

Purpose: Mindful listening and seeing, Focus

Best for: Ages 4+, groups or one-on-one

What you need: Room to move

The classic Simon Says game uses both mindful seeing and listening skills. When the leader (the designated Simon) issues her command verbally and shows what to do visually, kids are challenged to pay attention to both visual and auditory input and discern whether or not to act. The clue is that there's a conflict between what they see visually and what they are instructed to do verbally. Remember, you are only allowed to act when the leader says "Simon says" before the instruction. We tend to act without thinking, and this game demonstrates just that. Simon Says is a fun way to practice mindfulness by paying attention to outer experiences.

Here's how the game works. Choose who will take the role of Simon. It's best if you model it first.

Next, Simon stands in front of the player(s) and issues instructions for physical actions and shows how to do them. The instructions should be followed only if prefaced with the phrase "Simon says." Players win when they follow an instruction that is preceded by the phrase "Simon says." Players fail if they perform the action without the "Simon says" phrase or if they fail to perform the action when the phrase "Simon says" is used before the instruction.

If you want to keep the game less competitive, you don't have to eliminate players when they fail. When you play with just one child, you can decide to switch roles when the player fails three times. It doesn't matter if you can actually perform the physical tasks, an attempt is enough. The ability to distinguish fake commands is what matters in this fun game.

Here are some amusing examples:

- Simon says play air guitar. Simon demonstrates playing air guitar.
- Simons says waddle like a penguin. Simon does a penguin impression.
- Simon says cry like a baby. Simon cries like a baby.
- Simon says tickle your feet. Simon tickles his feet.
- Simon says giggle. Simon giggles.
- Simon says freeze. Simon freezes.
- Simon says spin around once. Simon spins around.

- Simon says spin around twice. Simon spins around twice.
- Spin around three times. Simon spins around thrice.

Did you attempt to spin around after this last command? If you spun around, you failed. Simon didn't say "Simon says" before the command. :-)

When you are done playing, talk about the experience. Ask your child if it was hard or easy to pay attention to the instructions. Was it hard to pay attention to the instructions when excited and having fun? Discuss how paying attention to what we see and hear could be helpful.

Mindful arms

Purpose: Body awareness, Mindful movement, Focus

Best for: Ages 4+, groups or one-on-one

What you need: Nothing except your body

This one is similar to the Flappy Bird activity, but perhaps a little easier to do. There are things that we do with our bodies every single day without giving them much thought. For children, especially school-aged children, one of those things is the motion of raising an arm in the air. If they aren't raising it to answer a question or get attention, they are reaching up to grab something or swing from a monkey bar. This exercise will let your child focus on this one body movement that they perform many times a day.

Have your child sit in a calm, quiet place where he will not be tempted to move around or fidget.

Have your child slowly raise one arm in the air. Talk him through the movement and work that his muscles are doing, and ask if he can feel his body working.

Have him leave his arm in the air for a few minutes, asking him to describe the different feelings in his arm as time goes by. Does his arm feel warm or heavy? Is it starting to shake or becoming difficult to keep in the air? Can he feel the strength of his muscles supporting it?

When you finally let him lower his arm, ask him to describe how it feels now and compare how it feels now to the way the raised arm felt.

Flappy bird
Purpose: Body awareness, Mindful movement, Focus

Best for: Ages 4+, groups or one-on-one

What you need: Somewhere to sit

This another great activity for active kids. It's probably a good idea to demonstrate this activity first by doing it yourself.

You can explain that paying attention to our bodies helps us in many ways. When we know how to move mindfully, we don't hurt people with our bodies and we don't hurt ourselves, like by running into something or somebody—or tripping.

Tell your child that we learn how to move mindfully by training to move slowly. If we are good at being mindful when we are slow, then we can practice mindful movement while we move more quickly.

To begin, ask your child to sit down. Sit still for twenty seconds and ask him to pay attention to how his body feels. Ask him to put his arms down to his side.

Guided script:
Slowly lift your arms, as if you were a bird flying.

Notice if your arms feels heavy or light.

Notice if the feeling changes as you slowly lift your arms like a big bird?

Now, lower your arms very slowly, paying attention to your arms.

Notice if your arms feel heavy or light.

Let's try it again, this time notice what temperature you feel— warm, cold, hot.

Notice if it changes when you flap your wings really slowly.

Slowly lift your wings up ... and ... down.

If it feels difficult for him, you can say that he can use anchor words to focus on the activity: "up" as he lifts his arms up and "down" as he lowers his arms. He can slowly repeat these words in sync with the activity.

Let's try it again. Now, fly slowly at your own pace and pay attention to any feelings in your body.

Can you feel the strength of your muscles supporting your arms?

Are your arms starting to shake a little?

Is it becoming difficult to keep up flying?

Notice if your arms feel heavy or light.

Notice if the feeling changes over time.

When you finally tell him to lower his arms, ask him to describe how it feels now. How does it feel to rest his arms compared to flying? Ask him why it is useful to be able to be mindful when we move?

Mindfulness of body

Purpose: Body awareness, Focus, Calm

Best for ages 4+, groups or one-on-one

What you need: A pleasant place

This is one of the simplest activities that you can do. Bring your child to a place she enjoys. This can be her bedroom, the back yard, a park, a lake, etc. While you want this to be a fun place, you also want it to be reasonably free of distractions.

Have your child sit in this place and begin to notice all of the sensations of her body. Is it warm? Can you feel the sun's warmth on your face? Is there water? What does it feel like to just dip your toes into it? Are you sitting on a bench? What does the pressure of the bench against the back of your legs feel like? Stop and notice these sensations. Take off your shoes and experience the ground with your bare feet. Close your eyes and notice the difference between walking on the grass and a small patch of earth. Notice that you know the difference because you can feel it, and think about how many times a day you are aware of these transitions but don't take the time to really notice them. Have fun with this exercise, and let your child be the explorer. See what different sensations she is able to notice that you overlooked.

Mindful steps

Purpose: Body awareness, Mindful movement, Focus

Best for: Ages 4+, groups or one-on-one

What you need: Space to walk

Some children have a hard time sitting still, so this activity is great for active kids. It's a fun alternative to sitting still. The idea is to pay attention to the body as we move. We place our attention to how our bodies move when we walk. We focus on each step as we move. This exercise can be exercised at any time we walk, and because of that it can easily be practiced to increase daily mindfulness.

Find a space where you can easily walk. Indoors, you can walk in a circle. You can even walk in place with itty bitty to no space, but it's probably less fun.

To begin, ask your child to balance on both feet evenly. To put his hands at his sides. Ask him to notice what it feels like to be standing. Can he feel his feet on the ground, his knees supporting his weight?

Tell your child to pay attention to his legs and feet. Ask him to lift his right foot up, and gently place it down. Lift his left foot up, and gently place it down.

Tell him to pay attention to his feet, ankles and knees. Ask him to bend his knees a little. How does that feel?

Ask him to stand up again and feel the difference.

Next begin to walk. Ask him to very slowly lift his right foot and move it forward and place it on the ground. Lift his left foot and place it down. Try a few steps like that. Like walking on egg shells or slow motion.

Continue walking slow and mindfully. Ask your child to pay attention to how his legs and feet feel as he walks. How it feels when he lifts his foot. How it feels when he places his foot down.

Ask him to walk a little faster. Can he feel his feet, legs and hips?

Then ask him to walk slower. Ask him to notice if there's a difference to how it feels. Is it easier to pay attention when he walks slow?

If it's hard for him to focus on the activity you can say that he can say "lift" and "place" in his mind when he lifts his foot and places it down (or simply up and down).

Try walking super slow.

Try walking backwards slowly.

Tell him that when his mind wanders, when he forgets to pay attention to his body, he can simply focus back again on his body by saying "up" and "down" as he moves his feet.

When ready, ask your child if he was able to feel his body—his feet, legs and hips. How does he feel now after the activity? Was it calming? Did he feel focused? Did he like it? Ask him when he could practice mindful walking? The hallway? At recess? Walking to or from school?

Happy and sad music

Purpose: Mindfulness of sounds, Understanding emotions, Focus

Best for: Ages 4+, groups or one-on-one

What you need: A selection of music

This activity helps children understand emotions. Choose songs that elicit different kinds of emotions. Play the songs one by one, and ask the kids if they think the song is happy or sad. Then ask them why they think that. What is it that makes the song happy or sad? Is it the pitch, the volume, the speed or the singers voice, or what the singer tells? Continue like this until you've tried all songs. This activity is a good introduction to the Liking The Music activity.

Balancing game

Purpose: Body awareness, Impulse control, Focus, Calm

Best for: Ages 4+, groups or one-to-one

What you need: Small objects like Lego pieces, somewhere to lie down, and a timer

The balancing game is a fun way to learn body awareness and impulse control. We like to play this with Lego pieces. The idea is to see how long your child can stay still lying down balancing objects on his or her body.

1. To begin, ask your child to lie down and take five deep breaths.
2. Next, place small objects, like Lego pieces or chips from a board game, on his body. Start with the legs, putting objects just above his ankles and knees, then on the back of his hands, on his arms, his shoulders, his forehead, and one last one on his chin. Seven objects are likely enough; you don't want to make it too hard for him.
3. Tell your child to lie very still and to not let the objects fall.
4. Start a timer and tell him that the game has started.
5. When the first object drops, stop the timer and announce his score. Congratulate your kid on whatever happened.

You can ask your kid to focus on his breath to see if it helps him to stay calm and still. Guide your kid to pay attention to his breath or allow him to do it alone. See how long he is able to stay still that way. With older children, you can let them try the game with their eyes open and closed. Tell them that they will likely notice that focusing on their breath with eyes closed helps them balance longer. With younger children, you want to first teach them how to pay attention to their breath.

6. When ready, ask your child if it was easy or hard. Did he like it? Was he able to feel the objects? Does he think it will get easier with practice? Did mindful breathing help him to score higher?

You can keep score and play this game as many times as he likes. You can track it and see if you improve over time (when you get used to mindful breathing, for example). If you want to, you can start playing without mindful breathing and add it later to show how it can improve focus.

Whatever you do, keep it playful. Play it yourself and let your kid keep time (if he's old enough). Maybe you can even get him to guide you through some mindful breathing when it's your time to play.

Unplug

Purpose: Awareness of surroundings, Engagement with surroundings, Focus, Calm

Best for ages 4+, groups or one-on-one

What you need: The great outdoors

Simply unplug from technology and spend time together. Go for a walk and point out things to your child that he may not have noticed before, and have him point out things to you. You might have noticed the different shades of pink of your neighbor's flowers but never once noticed the crack in the sidewalk that your child looks at each time he crosses it. Chances are your child sees the pebbles and random blades of grass that spring from it. He likely also knows that it is a favorite spot for ants to scurry through.

Your child notices an incredible amount of detail every day. Help him realize it by stopping to experience it with him.

Three senses

Purpose: Mindfulness of sounds, surroundings, and body, Focus, Calm

Best for: Ages 4+, groups or one-on-one

What you need: Nothing

It's hard to be frustrated and anxious when you are completely focused on your senses because you are fully engaged in the now, instead of stuck worrying about the future or caught in regrets. This is why mindfulness can be so liberating.

To begin, tell your child that he can focus on his senses to calm his body and mind. That you will pay attention to sound, sight, and touch to try this out. Explain that he will simply pay attention to his senses when you ask him questions. You can talk about what he noticed when you're done—and that he should try to be silent and pay attention during the activity. It's easier and more fun that way.

Next, take five slow breaths together and then ask your child:
1.What are three things you can hear?
2.What are three things you can see?
3.What are three things you can feel?
Give him about 30-60 seconds per question.

When you are done, ask him what he noticed per question. Perhaps he heard a clock, saw a painting, and felt the chair under him, and so on. With younger children, you may want to pause after each question. Finally, ask how this activity made him feel. Could he use this skill when he's bored or anxious? When would that be?

The next two activities will offer you some practical variations you can try out:

10 sounds

Purpose: Mindfulness of sounds, Focus, Calm

Best for: Ages 4+, groups or one-on-one

What you need: Nothing

Sometimes my three-year-old son Anton asks me and my wife Hanna to focus and discover ten different sounds at the dinner table. This is something he came up with after we tried Three Senses a few times. It's simple–it's just the listening part of the previous activity.

I was not going to share this, but it made all the parents laugh at one of my courses, so here it is… sometimes I add a little extra fun to the game by making fake fart noises when he concentrates really, really hard with his eyes closed. Obviously this is a lot of fun for a three-year-old :-) I've played this little sound game with my son while he sits on the toilet at least a hundred times.

Spot a color

Purpose: Mindfulness of surroundings, Focus, Calm

Best for: Ages 4+, groups or one-on-one

What you need: Nothing

Sometimes we play a game of "Spot a color." Which simply means that each person gets to choose a color in turn and the other player tries to find something in that color. Anton likes to play this on the toilet at night when he wants to slow down and when we wait for the train.

It goes like this:

"Try to find a red thing in this room ..."

"What are all the purple things you can see from where you sit?"

You can play this at the grocery store too, just ask your kid to find something and fetch it for you:

"Can you find something yellow that begins with a B?"

You can ask your child to help you pick groceries like this or simply play a game and ask him or her to return the stuff back to the shelves.

Attention to detail
Purpose: Detail awareness, Recognizing everyday beauty, Focus, Calm

Best for ages 5+, groups or one-on-one

What you need: Any nature-based object that you can see or touch

This exercise is best when done outside, but it doesn't need to be; it can be done anywhere that you and your child are comfortable. You want to pick just one object, one that is found in nature that you have seen many times and can easily recognize, but that is also just slightly different from others like it. Examples are flowers, clouds, pinecones, stones, etc.

Take an object with your child and quietly reflect on it. Notice all of the unique details in this item as if it were the first time that you have ever seen it. What do you notice that you never noticed before? How is it different from or the same as others? Try this with a new object each day.

What I notice about you
Purpose: Detail awareness, Focus, Connection, Calm

Best for ages 5+, groups or one-on-one

What you need: Nothing

This exercise helps children learn focus on what they see—it's a fun activity to see how much more we can notice when we pay attention. It also helps kids practice social skills and connect with their peers.

If you are with a group of kids, pair them up to do the activity. Guide each pair through the activity one pair at a time. If you practice with one child, then do this activity together with her. You can model by going first. Observe your child for 30 seconds and then share something about her: "I see your eyes are green," "I see your shirt is pink," "I see you have no socks on," or "I saw you smile at me."

Now it's your kid's turn. Ask your child to spend 30 seconds watching you. Ask her to pay attention to something about you, as if it was the first time that they see you. After 30 seconds, ask her to share something she noticed.

Do a few rounds of this. When you are done, ask your child how it felt and if they noticed something that hadn't before.

The mindful smile - a mini body scan
Purpose: Body awareness, Focus, Calm

Best for: Ages 5+, groups or one-on-one

What you need: Somewhere to sit or lie down comfortably

The mindful smile helps children (and adults) cultivate focusing skills and body awareness. This activity is similar to the Body Scan but focuses only on the face. It has a calming effect and is really nice to do.

To begin, ask your child to lie down comfortably and close her eyes. Alternatively, she can keep her eyes in a soft gaze. It may be easier to do this exercise eyes closed, however. Explain that it's best to just focus on her smile when you ask her questions— she's not supposed to answer you—and that you can talk about it all when you have finished.

Guided script:
Take a deep breath and pay attention to your body.

Now, slowly turn your mouth up into a smile—a normal smile you might give to someone you like. You can pretend that you see someone you like. That someone smiles at you. And you smile back.

If this feels funny—that's great.

Notice how your lips feel. Are your lips closed together or apart? Just notice.

Is your mouth open? How does your mouth and tongue feel? Where is your tongue placed?

Now, pay attention to your cheeks. How does your smile make your cheeks feel? Does your smile push them up? Are your cheeks warm or cool?

Pay attention to your eyes. Does your smile change anything about your eyes? Do your eyes feel like they are smiling? Do your cheeks push the corners of your eyes upwards?

Have you noticed that sometimes when someone smiles at you it makes you smile too? You can often notice a smile like that in the eyes of the person that smiles at you. It looks like their eyes are smiling too.

Now pay attention to the rest of your face. How does your face feel when you smile? How about your ears? Are they smiling?

How about your jaw? Is it tight or loose?

What about your forehead? Is it smooth or something else?

Now pay attention to your whole body for a short while. Can you notice any sensations?

Well done. When you are ready, slowly get up.

When you are finished, tell your child that they can practice this in bed if they like it. They could start a day with a smile like this, or go to sleep smiling. Wouldn't that be fun to try out?

Liking the music
Purpose: Mindfulness of sounds, Focus

Best for: Ages 5+, groups or one-on-one

What you need: A selection of music

This activity helps kids learn mindful listening skills while enjoying music. The idea is to teach kids to focus on sounds and to notice a range of detail.

Pick a mix of music that fits the age of your child or group of children. With adolescents, you might want to first ask them what they'd like to listen to. Trying out different genres from country to rock, classical to jazz, is a fun way to identify differences in the styles and how they affect their feelings. Be sure to listen to the music beforehand so that you can plan what you want them to notice.

The game is simple. You play a song and ask them to pay attention to the song. Here are a few different ideas you might want to try out:

Ask them to listen to the song and give a thumbs up (likes) when they ...

- hear a specific instrument,
- hear drums start beating,
- hear drums stop beating,
- hear the voice of a singer start or stop,
- hear a specific word,
- notice that the music affects their feelings,
- feel uplifted by the music,
- feel calmed by the music,
- feel the music make them feel sad or anxious.

Pick just one or two things per song.

You can also ask them to listen and pay attention to their feelings. After the music stops, ask them how the music made them feel. This is a great way to learn how to notice and talk about emotions.

When you are done listening to music, ask them if it was easy to stay focused. Were they able to bring their attention back to the music if their minds wandered? Were they able to notice whatever it was you chose to have them pay attention to?

Balancing relay
Purpose: Body awareness, Focus

Best for: Ages 5+, groups or one-on-one

What you need: A spoon and some water (or a spoon and a potato) per team

Similar to the egg-and-spoon race, this game teaches both focus and body awareness. The idea is to carry a spoon full of water to the next kid without spilling a drop. You can make it into a relay race if you are playing with a group of kids. To take it to the next level, ask your child to walk backwards or sideways while balancing the spoon.

Hawk-eyes

Purpose: Mindful seeing, Detail awareness, Connection with surroundings, Focus

Best for: Ages 5+, groups or one-on-one

What you need: Nothing

This simple activity helps children sharpen their focus and calm down. When we pay attention to our senses we allow our minds to calm down. This exercise is a nice alternative to mindful breathing, especially if your child has asthma or a negative association to breathing. Mindful seeing is a helpful skill. Paying attention to visual input allows the brain to find detail and novelty in ordinary situations. Children learn to pay attention to their surroundings while recognizing details, like a friends' mood, becomes easier.

You can do this activity anywhere, but it's nice to try out at home somewhere where we are used to the setting and might think there's nothing new to notice.

Begin by telling your child to use his hawk eyes to scan the room. Tell him to pretend to be a hawk (or a lion, his favorite superhero, etc.) and to move his head very slowly, looking very carefully at the space. Ask him to take in the details.

Finally, ask him to notice something in the room that he hasn't noticed before. Spend about a minute scanning the room, then let him share what he noticed.

Ask him if he noticed something he hadn't before, or something that he had forgotten about. Ask him if he thinks this skill could be useful and how he'd use it.

Mindful eyes

Purpose: Mindful seeing, Detail awareness, Connection with surroundings, Focus

Best for: Ages 5+, groups or one-on-one

What you need: Nothing

Pick something natural within your immediate environment and ask your kid to focus on just that for a minute or two. It could be a flower, a flame, a bee, the clouds, or the moon. Ask them to focus only on that one object, to observe it as if they were seeing it for the first time.

Dance, dance, dance

Purpose: Body awareness, Mindfulness of emotions, Focus

Best for: Ages 5+, groups or one-on-one

What you need: a few different songs, dancing room

Dancing is a great way to let go of our inner chatter. When we get immersed in dance we forget our worries and regrets, and our minds calm down. Kids love to dance, and I recommend all adults dance more. This activity is a lot of fun and it's simple.

Older children and teens (and grown-ups too) often need to be reminded that there's no right or wrong way to dance—that they should let go of any ideas of how to look cool and just go with the feeling. One way to accomplish this is to close their eyes.

Remember to dance, too. Do it together and have fun. Choose a few different tunes so that you can ask your child how different types of music makes them feel. Try to find songs that elicit different feelings. Songs with different beats and moods. You can ask your child beforehand what music he likes and include that too.

1. To begin, ask your child to listen to the music for a while. Then ask him to move with the music slowly—and finally to dance if he so wishes.
2. Tell him to feel the music and pay attention to how the music makes his body feel as he moves.

   Ask him if he can feel the music in his body.
3. After each song, ask your child how it made him feel and if he can pinpoint where he felt emotions.

When you're done with all songs, ask him if there was a difference in how the songs made him feel.

Mindful feet - a mini body scan

Purpose: Body awareness, Focus, Calm

Best for: Ages 5+, groups or one-on-one

What you need: Nothing

You can start by asking your child to remove her shoes to make the activity even more relaxing. Then ask your child to sit or stand relaxed with both feet firmly on the ground.

Ask her to breathe normally and take a moment to notice how she is feeling right now. This exercise is easier to do if you close your eyes, so ask your child to close her eyes if she feels comfortable doing so.

Then ask her to bring her attention to the soles of her feet by pushing them softly against the ground for a short moment.

Ask her to pay attention to her feet, how they make contact with the ground and possibly her shoes. How does it feel? Soft or hard? Can she feel her socks? Give her time to focus and investigate.

Continue to ask her questions: How do her heels feel? Her toes? Can she feel the space between her toes? Ask her to move her toes a little bit and try again. Locate each toe individually by having her pay attention to them one by one.

Be curious. Ask if her feet are warm or cold. If you happen to be outside, is there a slight breeze to be felt on the skin? A tingling sensation somewhere?

Simply ask her to rest her attention at her feet—to pay attention to her feet. See if she can have her mind think about her feet and nothing else.

If your child is sitting down, you can expand the exercise to include the contact points between her and the chair. Can she feel the chair under her? How about her back resting against the chair?

Keep the exercise short, but give your child enough time to focus and get immersed. End by asking her how she feels, and if she can think of any situations when this exercise could be useful. Is she more focused and more calm after the exercise? Could she consider doing it just before a test to calm down?

Balancing on one foot
Purpose: Body awareness, Focus

Best for: Ages 5+, groups or one-on-one

What you need: Nothing

This is a simple game to develop focus and body awareness. It can be used to combat boredom while standing in a line, for example. Ask your child to focus her gaze on a point slightly below eye level. Then ask her to stand on one leg and keep her gaze on the focal point. How long can she balance like this? Try the other leg. To make it more difficult, engage your child in conversation or ask her to sing something or to balance with her eyes closed. With a group of kids, you can see who can balance the longest.

Pass the cup

Purpose: Body awareness, Impulse Control, Connection, Focus

Best for: Ages 6+, groups or one-on-one

What you need: A cup filled with water and a spill-friendly floor

Pass the cup is a fun game to sharpen concentration and build body awareness. Find a cup that is unbreakable (as it might fall) and fill it to about an inch from the rim. Depending on the age of the child, you can fill the cup just right to give them a fair chance to succeed. If you are doing this with a group of kids, you may want to sit or stand in a circle. You can play this one-on-one too.

To begin, tell your child that the idea is to pass the cup to one another without spilling water. Tell her that we do this by looking at the cup and the next person that is about to receive it. We also have to move slowly and feel with our hands.

Next, give the cup to her and ask her to pass it forward slowly (to the next kid or yourself). Have fun and enjoy it.

After you've passed the cup a few times, it's time to try it without talking. Ask her how that could be different, if maybe she needs to pay closer attention to the person she passes the cup to.

Do a round if you have a group of kids, or pass it back and forth a few times if you're doing the activity with just one kid.

Finally, it's time to try passing the cup silently with eyes closed. Tell your child that she needs to be extra careful with her eyes closed, and that paying attention to sounds and touch is even more important now.

Pass the cup a few times.

When ready, ask how it was. Was it easy or hard? Did something make her lose her concentration? What was it? How was it different with her eyes closed?

Do just one thing
Purpose: Present-mindedness, Focus, Calm

Best for: Ages 6+, groups or one-on-one

What you need: Nothing

Try this exercise on yourself first, and then explain the exercise to your child on his terms. It could be something like this:

Try every day to do something fully immersed. For example, when walking to school, don't think about doing your chores, think about walking one step at a time. During chores, don't think about football practice, think about the chore you are doing. If you are washing the dishes, wash the dishes. See the color of the plate, the smell of the soap, the feel of the water, the sound of glasses clinking together. And during football training, focus on just that, not what you're planning to do with your friends. And when you are with your friends, be with your friends. Be. Be now. Don't let your life be a dream of what will happen or what has happened. Let life be now, right now. Be here in this moment.

This is actually much more difficult than you might expect it to be. A major focus of mindfulness practice is being fully present and not letting our minds wander too much to things in the past that we cannot change, or worrying too much about the future. When we concentrate intently on the now, we eliminate a significant amount of stress and worry. This is a valuable lifelong skill that takes time to develop, and it's an excellent exercise to work on together with your child.

Jenga

Purpose: Body awareness, Understanding emotions, Focus

Best for: Ages 6+, groups or one-on-one

What you need: Jenga the game (or similar)

Jenga isn't just for kids–it's a lot of fun for everyone. It teaches you how to pay attention, too. You can make it mindful by asking your child to pay attention to whatever it is that distracts her from the game.

Is she able to notice what made her lose focus?

Did thoughts or emotions make her lose concentration?

How about if you ask her tough questions as you play?

See how the game changes when you find a calm and clear mind. Try a few mindful breaths (or another focusing activity) and see how it affects the results.

Mindfulness touch point

Purpose: Awareness, Focus, Calm

Best for: Ages 6+, groups or one-on-one

What you need: Nothing

This activity will help you to introduce more mindfulness throughout your child's day. Think of a place at home that can act as a mindfulness trigger – a reminder to pause and calm down. It could be the bathroom door knob or the fridge or a painting. You could craft a STOP sign or a painting to remind you. Make a game of it during the first few days and count how many times each one has noticed to pause. Every time you touch the knob (for example), pause, take a deep breath, and notice how you feel bringing yourself to the present moment.

Pennies game
Purpose: Detail awareness, Focus, Calm

Best for: Ages 6+, groups or one-on-one

What you need: One penny for each player, a basket

Everyone gets a penny and a minute to study it in detail. The pennies are then placed back in the basket. Each player has to pick their penny out of all the pennies and say how they knew it was theirs. This game can be played with different objects, too.

Stay cool
Purpose: Body awareness, Impulse control, Focus

Best for: Ages 6+, groups

What you need: Nothing

Now this is a fun game to try out with a group. The idea is that the players try to sit still and quiet. The last person remaining still wins the competition. You can facilitate the game like this:

1. Ask everyone to sit down and stay still for as long as they can. The players are allowed to blink. But they are not allowed to hide their faces. It's nice to sit in a circle since you

get to see everyone's reactions and it can be a lot of fun to see players lose their cool.

2. Your job is to watch the players and call out each player who moves or makes a sound.

3. The last one remaining still and quiet wins.

4. Repeat the game for 3-5 rounds.

TIP: You can make the game funnier by taunting the players with a fun commentary, if you like.

"I see that Allison is having a hard time staying cool. She's smiling already. And Peter looks like his head will explode any time now. Who will win? Allison or Peter?"

TIP: Teach the whole group a few mindfulness techniques they can apply to stay calm during the game, and see if it helps. For example, sensory awareness techniques like focusing on their sight, i.e., gazing at one object in the room. Or focusing on their breath or their feet pressing against the floor. Or the sounds outside.

7 and up

Waiting game

Purpose: Mindfulness of sounds and surroundings, Impulse control, Focus, Calm

Best for: Ages 7+, groups or one-on-one

What you need: Nothing

When was the last time you and your child had to wait? I'm sure you've had plenty of opportunity to wait. We wait in line at the cafeteria, in traffic, waiting for our spouse, parent or child. Ask your kid how waiting makes her feel. Explain to her how it's easy to get anxious when waiting, but that we can focus on our surroundings to calm down and perhaps even enjoy those moments. Sometimes we miss out on beautiful things when we worry.

Ask if she experiences anxiousness when waiting. Is there something that repeats often, like waiting for the bus, for her parents, or something at school or somewhere else?

Next, tell her that you can train mindful waiting together and that she can try it out the next time she's anxious or frustrated waiting for something (even if it's for you).

Begin the exercise by sitting down or standing still. Tell your child to pick something pleasant to look at. Tell her to hold her focus on the object. You don't have to strain your eyes; instead try to find a soft gaze. Ask her to be curious about the object and to inspect all the details.

Ask her if she notices any thoughts. Maybe she thinks it's not working or she's bored. Tell her that it's okay. That's exactly how it feels when waiting—and noticing she's distracted is exactly what being mindful is!

Tell her that when thoughts come, it's okay—she can let them be and focus on the object again. Let her focus on the object for a minute and congratulate her for a good job.

Ask her how it felt. Did time go slow or fast when she focused on the object. Did she notice thoughts or emotions? Does she think this could work for her in the future? Tell her that she could try it out when she's waiting the next time.

Rub your pants
Purpose: Body awareness, Focus, Calm

Best For: Ages 7+, groups or one-on-one

What you need: Nothing

This simple and practical activity will help your kid tune in to their senses for a short while. Tuning in to their senses like this can help them focus and calm down.

Ask your kid to sit down and to place his hands palms-down on his thighs. Then slowly rub his pants in one direction. Ask him to feel the fabric of his pants. What's the texture like? Is it warm or cool? After about 30 seconds, ask him to rub his pants in the opposite direction and to feel the fabric again. After 30 seconds, tell him to stop and ask him how he feels. Was it calming? It often is—even if this activity can feel silly at first.

12 and up

Body scan for older children
Purpose: Body awareness, Focus, Calm, Relaxation

Best for: Ages 12+, groups or one-on-one

What you need: Somewhere to sit or lie down comfortably, 5 to 10 minutes

This activity guides your child to pay attention to his body, starting from his toes all the way to his head. The exercise has a calming and relaxing effect, and it builds focusing skills. It can help us notice emotions and other sensations in our bodies, too.

The first time you attempt this with your child, ask him to lie down; make sure he's wearing comfortable clothes and the room isn't too hot or too cold. Tell him to pay attention to how different parts of his body feel, moving up the body from his toes to his head as the activity progresses.

Guided script:
Focus your attention on your breath. You don't have to change

your breath. Just notice it and feel it in your body.

If you want to, you can close your eyes.

You may notice air going in and coming out again by the tip of your nose. What do you notice when you direct your attention there to the tip of your nose?

You may notice your breath in your chest, too. What do you notice when you direct your attention there? Does it expand when you breathe in? Does it contract when you breathe out?

Now, place both hands on your stomach. Draw a few normal slow breaths. Can you feel your hands move up and down with your breath?

Wherever you feel your breath is okay.

Place your hands back at your side.

Bring your attention to your body and notice what it feels like to be lying down.

Feel how the floor or bed supports you.

Feel the points of contact between your body and the bed, or floor.

Next you'll be bringing your attention up through the body, starting at your feet and going all the way up to your head.

Now gently bring your attention to your feet. If you're finding it hard to feel your feet, you can gently wiggle your toes.

Explore the sensations that you feel at your toes and feet. Some sensations are obvious, such as contact between your feet and the floor, or even your socks or clothing touching your skin. Others are more subtle, like itching or tingling sensations or warmth or the air brushing against your skin. You might notice different temperatures. Just notice the different sensations at your feet.

Now, move your attention up into your legs: your calves, your knees, your thighs. Become aware of both your legs and the sensations. You might find that there's a lot to feel in this area, or you may not feel much at all.

Now bring your attention to your hips, your buttocks, your lower back, and feel where your body makes contact with the floor or bed.

You might find that your mind wanders off and gets distracted and you're no longer paying attention to the sensations in your body. It's completely normal if this happens. Every time you find that your mind has wandered, bring your attention gently back to scanning your body.

Now, very gently, move your attention up into your stomach. Just notice what you feel there. Is it tight? Is it loose and relaxed? Can you feel your belly move up and down with your breath? Simply notice this area of the body.

Now, very gently, bring your attention up to your chest. You might notice the movement of your breath or the feeling of your clothes on your skin.

Now, move your attention up into your shoulders and neck. This is often a place where stress is held; just notice.

Explore the sensations of your arms, hands, and each of your fingers. How do they feel? Is there heat? Tingling? Tightness? What other sensations do you notice here?

Lastly, bring your attention up to your head, into your face, starting with the forehead, noticing if there's tightness there or if it feels relaxed.

Bring your attention to your eyes. What do they feel in their sockets right now? Notice the tissue that surrounds the eyes. Is there strain there? Is it relaxed?

Bring your attention down into your cheekbones, your jaw, and your mouth.

If you wish, you can open your attention to your full body, noticing it in its entirety.

Expand your attention so it includes your whole body. What do you feel?

When it's over, ask your child how it felt and how he feels now. You can start with the "Squish and let go" exercise to get used to body sensations.

Mindful Breathing

Mindful breathing is just another sensory awareness technique. I chose to highlight it like this because it's likely the most popular way to practice mindfulness. Grown-up practitioners use this technique, and so do kindergarteners.

Kids often say it makes them feel good. After even a few sessions, your kid may find that they are more focused, calmer, and more relaxed. This is the technique we use the most with my son. Mindful breathing is something we do at least a few times per week. Some weeks, we practice daily. When we practice together with my four-year-old son, we practice only for a minute or so. The shortest variations of mindful breathing in this book take only about 60 seconds to complete, so time will not be an issue if you like the practice.

The practice has the power to make you feel more focused and calmer. The way I got my son to understand the benefits of mindful breathing was this: I started to practice it myself at times when I knew it would benefit me... and my son, indirectly. And I made sure to point it out to my son.

He saw firsthand how the practice helped me and how it changed the way we interacted. I could cool down and be more patient with him when I was tired and frustrated. I could focus on the badminton game we were playing together, instead of fumbling because my mind was busy thinking about work. I could be present at the breakfast table, slow down, and enjoy the meal, instead of worrying about work emails. I could focus and become less anxious... and leave my smartphone alone when I was bored.

He saw how I developed impulse control and how I could be more present. Kids are smart, and when they see how practice affects you, they will want the same superpowers.

How does mindful breathing work? You pay attention to your breath—how it feels in your body to breathe. This focuses your mind, and your mind gets to rest. Mindful breathing is paying attention to your body to give your mind something to focus on. When you focus on your breath, your mind has a chance to rest from all the thoughts that occupy it—be it worries about the future or negative experiences from the past.

You simply pay attention to how it feels in your body when you breathe. How your belly goes gently up and down when you breathe. Or how you might feel the air go in and out of your nostrils. Or how your lungs and chest expand and contract.

Don't worry if, for some reason, your kid doesn't like mindful breathing. If your child has asthma or a negative association to breathing you may want to try another sensory awareness technique that focuses on touch, taste, smell or sight. Some kids (and adults) prefer to pay attention to sounds, and some like to do a short body scan to focus and calm down. The mechanism is the same—we shift our focus to our senses.

This is what you can learn through practice:

1. Paying attention to your breath is calming.
2. Focusing is a skill you can train yourself to do.
3. You have the power to focus on what you want to focus on... and perform better.
4. Focusing on your breath helps you to manage difficult thoughts and emotions.

WARNING!

BE SURE NOT TO MISS SOME OF THE BEST ACTIVITIES.

Please don't let the age recommendations restrict you.

The age recommendations are more about how difficult the exercises are than what age they are most suited for. So, for example, "3 and up" activities work fine for a teen or a grown-up, but "12 and up" activities are most likely too advanced for children under the age of six. "3 and up" activities are often great for older kids, teens, and even grown-ups. And you might want to start with some of them to introduce mindfulness in a super-easy way regardless of age.

3 and up

Breath cause and effect

Purpose: Body awareness, Mindfulness of breath, Focus

Best for: Ages 3+, one-on-one

What you need: Bubbles, a pinwheel, cotton ball, feather or other object that a child can move by blowing

This is a great way to help a very young child develop awareness of his breathing. To begin, give your child the object (or let him choose one if you have more than one), and ask him to inhale deeply. On the exhale – he should take his time with it – tell him to watch what happens to the object. For example, if it's a cotton ball on a table, how far did it go? If he used a pinwheel, how many turns did it make? Continue the process, perhaps asking the child to complete more slow breaths in succession before stopping to discuss.

Blowing bubbles
Purpose: Body awareness, Mindfulness of breath, Focus, Calm

Best for: Ages 3+, groups or one-on-one

What you need: Soap bubbles

Try blowing bubbles. It's a fun way to take a first step towards mindful breathing, to practice deep breathing, and to develop awareness of breath. Ask your child to inhale slowly and blow a big bubble. The bigger the bubble, the deeper the breath will be. Experiment with fast and slow breathing and different-sized bubbles, and explain that a few deep breaths can help us calm down. Ask your child how it feels after some deep breathing. It will take some time to grasp this concept, but something like this gives you a foundation, one that is also fun for both of you.

Snuggle meditation
Purpose: Body awareness, Mindfulness of breath, Focus, Calm

Best for: Ages 3+, one-on-one

What you need: Gentle music if you wish

This is a lovely meditation to do with your child. Put on some soothing music and find a nice place to sit with your child. Sit with him in your lap with his back against your belly. First ask him to pay attention to the music or something that you both can observe in front of you. Maybe you're sitting at a window and you can guide him to look at whatever happens outside – the trees, the sky or the cars driving by. When your kid is comfortable, tell him that you can both calm down by paying attention to your breath. That you can actually feel your own breath come in and go out. Tell him that he can start by feeling your breath. Wouldn't that be fun? Ask him to notice if he can feel your belly as you breath in and out. Take some slow deep breaths and ask how it feels on his back when you breathe. Is your belly warm? Does it go in and out slowly? Sit like this for a short while and then instruct your child to place his hands on his own tummy. Ask him if he can feel his belly go up and down as he breathes in and out. If it feels hard at first, you can take a few deep breaths.

When you're ready, ask your child how it made him feel.

Blowing the candle
Purpose: Body awareness, Mindfulness of breath, Focus, Calm

Best for: Ages 3+, groups or one-on-one

What you need: Somewhere to sit

This activity teaches your child how focusing on his breath can calm him down.

Guided script:
Close your eyes and imagine you're holding a candle in your right hand.

Breathe out slowly to make the candle flame wiggle. But be careful not to blow it out yet.

Now breathe in slowly and fill your lungs.

Breathe out slowly to make the candle flame wiggle. Just enough so that you make the candle wiggle. We don't want to blow it out.

Take another breath at your own pace and breathe out gently toward your candle.

Do two more breaths really slow and be gentle not to blow the flame out.

Well done. Now you can take one more big breath and blow the candle flame out.

When you are done, ask him how it felt to focus like that. Was it fun? How does his body feel? How about his thoughts? Are they calmer? Explain that breathing on purpose like this can help ones' thoughts and body calm down.

Hot chocolate
Purpose: Body awareness, Mindfulness of breath, Focus, Calm

Best for: Ages 3+, groups or one-on-one

What you need: Somewhere to sit

With "Hot chocolate" we learn how focusing on a long out-breath can be calming. This activity is a great way to show how paying attention to our breath helps us focus and calm down.

Sit down and ask your child to make a cup out of his hands and pretend it's a delicious cup of hot chocolate. Tell him that it tastes so good that he wants to drink it this instant, but it's still too hot. To cool it down a bit, he will blow on it with a long out-breath.

Let him try it a few times, then tell him that he can make the out-breath even longer. Tell him that you will help him by counting when he breathes, like this: Breathing in—one, two. Breathing out—one, two, three, and four.

Breathe for 30 to 60 seconds like this. Adjust to his natural breathing rhythm and count: Breathing in—one, two. Breathing out—one, two, three, and four.

After 30-60 seconds tell him that the chocolate is cool. Tell him to take a sip, and say "Mmm."

Ask him how he feels and explain that breathing on purpose like this can help his mind and body calm down.

Take five

Purpose: Body awareness, Mindfulness of breath, Focus, Calm

Best for: Ages 3+ groups or one-on-one

What you need: Nothing

This is my favorite, and I use it every week on my own and with my son. It's great for kids, teens, and grown-ups, too. After a few tries, your kid can use this calming strategy independently. Here's how it works:

- Simply make a fist of your preferred hand and open one finger at a time when you've completed one breath cycle (following one in-breath and one out-breath all the way).
- You breathe in and notice the air going in.
- You breathe out and extend your first finger. This is take one.
- Gently take another breath. Notice the air going in.
- Breathe out and extend your second finger.

- When you've opened your palm fully, you know you're done! You can do this before a test, with your hand hidden under the table if you wish, or before a soccer game to calm yourself.

Blowing dandelions

Purpose: Body awareness, Mindfulness of breath, Focus, Calm

Best for: Ages 3+, groups or one-on-one

What you need: Somewhere to sit

This exercise is similar to the Take Five exercise. If you have blown dandelion puffballs with your child, this activity will be clearer. The idea is to use the five fingers of a hand as a visual aid for counting five breaths. The added benefit of this mindful breathing activity is that younger children will easily remember the idea of smelling and blowing dandelions. It's probably good to model this before you do it together.

Guided script:
Lift your hand, either one, closer to your face so that you can look at your fingers.

Imagine that each finger is a beautiful yellow dandelion. You'll soon get to smell each one.

Let's start with your thumb. Smell the first flower by bringing the top of your thumb/dandelion to your nose and smelling it. Can you feel your thumb touch your nose? Can you feel the air entering your nose as you inhale? (Spend a little time trying this out with the first finger.)

Well done. The flower has now turned into a puffball.

Now, blow on the top of your thumb to disperse the puffball. Do you feel your breath on your thumb as you breathe out? Does it feel cool or warm?

Now smell and blow the rest of the flowers however slow or fast you like; breathing in and smelling—touching each flower with your nose; breathing out and blowing the puffball—feeling the breath on your finger.

When ready, ask him how it felt to do it and how he is feeling now.

Balloon breathing with belly-breathing

Purpose: Body awareness, Mindfulness of breath, Focus, Calm

Best for: Ages 3+, groups or one-on-one

What you need: Somewhere to sit

This is similar to Teddy Bear Belly-Breathing. You can try out both exercises and see which one your child prefers. Ask your child to lie down on his back, extend his legs, and make sure he feels comfortable. You can use the following script with your child.

Guided script:
Imagine you have a balloon in your belly that you want to blow up.

Put your hands on your belly.

Close your eyes and picture that balloon. What color is it?

Now slowly inhale through your nose and inflate your belly balloon slowly. With your hands on your belly, feel that balloon filling up.

Slowly let the air out of your balloon through your mouth. Ahhh. Feel the balloon getting smaller.

Try again, breathing through your nose, slowly inflate your balloon and feel it growing as your belly rises.

Let the air out and feel the balloon getting smaller.

Do this exercise for five to ten breaths.

Ask your child how it felt and what he noticed during the session. Is there a difference in how he feels afterwards?

The star aka tracing five fingers

Purpose: Body awareness, Mindfulness of breath, Focus, Calm

Best for: Ages 4+ groups or one-on-one

What you need: Nothing

After a few tries, your child can use this calming strategy independently. Here's how it works:

Tell your child to fan out his hand "like a star,"(open his palm and spread his fingers) and place it on a table, a knee or some other surface.

Next, direct him to take his pointer finger from the opposite hand and begin to trace along the hand that is fanned out. Tell him to inhale through the nose as he traces the outside of his thumb, then exhale through the mouth as he traces along the inside of his thumb. Inhale as he traces the outside of his pointer finger, exhale as he traces the inside of his pointer finger... and so on and so forth until all of his fingers have been traced.

As he traces each finger, encourage him not only to focus on every breath but also to consider how the small movements feel on his hands.

When he is finished, ask him how it felt. Is he a tiny bit calmer, perhaps?

If combining breathing with tracing of the fingers feels like too much, then start with tracing only, and add synchronized breathing later. Even the act of tracing can help your child to focus on his senses and calm down.

Beach ball breathing

Purpose: Body awareness, Mindfulness of breath, Focus, Calm

Best for: Ages 4+, groups or one-on-one

What you need: Nothing

This calming activity is something I like to do myself, and my son likes it as well. It's simple and easy to remember, too.

You simply ask your child to pretend they are holding a big beach ball with both hands in front of them. Then you ask them to pull their hands apart as they breathe in—pretending the ball grows bigger. And as they breathe out, ask them to bring their hands back together—pretending the beach ball shrinks.

This activity helps them to learn mindful breathing—to pay attention to their breath and synchronize their arm movements with their breath.

Teddy bear belly-breathing aka breathing buddies

Purpose: Body awareness, Mindfulness of breath, Focus, Calm

Best for: Ages 4+, groups or one-on-one

What you need: Comfortable clothes, ample floor space (or another place to lie down), a favorite stuffed toy

Teddy bear belly-breathing works for two reasons.

1. When we concentrate intently on the now instead of on our mind chatter, we eliminate a significant amount of stress and worry. We shift our focus away from our thoughts and emotions.

2. Deep belly-breathing signals the nervous system to relax, which then lowers stress and reduces the heart rate and blood pressure.

To practice belly-breathing, ask your child to lie comfortably and place his hands on his belly. (If he uses a stuffed animal, he can hold it on top of his belly.)

As you count to three, ask him to inhale deeply through his nose. Tell him to fill his belly with air as he inhales; he should feel it get bigger and bigger and bigger through the count to three. If his stuffed toy sits on top of his belly, he might see it rise as his belly "fills with air."

Ask him to exhale to a slow count to four. Tell him he might see his toy fall as he feels his belly shrinking and shrinking through the count to four.

Do five to ten rounds of guided belly-breathing to get started.

Continue to belly-breathe for as long as he likes, and let him breathe at his own pace without the instructions. You can put on soothing music to help your child keep calm for the duration.

When ready, ask your child how it felt. Is there a difference in how he feels now? What did he notice about the stuffed animal as he inhaled and exhaled?

Heartful breathing
Purpose: Body awareness, Mindfulness of breath, Focus, Calm

Best for: Ages 5+, groups or one-on-one

What you need: Nothing

This is another simple and fun activity that teaches your child to pay attention to sensations in her body.

Guided script:
Take two deep breaths.

Now, place your hands over your heart. Notice how it feels.

Close your eyes gently.

Maybe you can feel your hands warming your chest.

Good.

Now, pay attention to your chest. Notice if you can feel your chest rise and fall as you breathe in and out.

Breathe like this for a short while and simply pay attention to how it feels to breathe.

Good job!

When ready, talk about how it felt. Did she notice any other sensations in her body? Did emotions or thoughts distract her? Was it nice? Was it calming?

Noticing breath
Purpose: Body awareness, Mindfulness of breath, Focus, Calm

Best for: Ages 5+, groups or one-on-one

What you need: Nothing

With this exercise, we focus on the child making a connection between his body and the act of breathing. It is a simple connection that we all take for granted. Breath awareness is one of the most accessible mindfulness techniques. We can learn to notice our breath and to rest our attention on our sensations.

Take a simple and lighthearted approach to helping your child become more aware of the breath/body connection with this guided exercise.

Begin by having your child find a comfortable place where he will be able to either lie down or sit with a straight back, so that he will be able to feel the breath moving in his body.

Guided script:
Now, gently close your eyes, and place both of your hands on your belly.

Take one really deep breath.

Now take two more.

How did that feel?

Let's do it again, and each time you breathe in, picture your breath coming into your body and filling up your belly.

See if you can you notice your belly move.

Good.

Now breathe normally.

See if you can still feel your hands moving up and down on your belly as you breathe.

When you are trying to pay attention to your belly moving when you breathe, you might get distracted. This is ok, and it happens to everybody. When this happens, do three big breaths, and focus on feeling your belly move up and down.

When ready, ask your child how it felt to focus on his breath. Ask him to notice how he feels after the exercise. How does his body feel now? Did he become a little calmer, more relaxed or even a little happier?

The point of this exercise is to learn to recognize and focus on breathing patterns. Feeling the breath enter and leave the belly is often the easiest way for children to make these associations. However, if your child is having trouble deep breathing and feeling the breath in his belly, you can try having him place a hand near his mouth, his nose or on his chest to begin with until he is able to notice his breath.

Finding your breath

Purpose: Body awareness, Mindfulness of breath, Focus, Calm

Best for: Ages 5+, groups or one-on-one

What you need: Nothing

This is similar to the Noticing Breath activity. The idea is to simply see how breathing feels in your body and where exactly it can be felt. Paying attention to the breath has a focusing and calming effect.

Guided script:
Take five slow breaths right now. Feel each breath from start to finish. Take it slow and put all of your curiosity into it.

Can you feel your breath in your nose, belly or chest?

Does your belly go up and down?

Does your chest expand and contract?

Can you feel your breath at the tip of your nose?

Good job!

How did this make you feel?

Counting to ten

Purpose: Body awareness, Mindfulness of breath, Focus, Calm

Best for: Ages 6+, groups or one-on-one

What you need: Nothing

Before counting breaths with your child, make sure he knows the difference between an inhale and an exhale. You can refer to the Noticing Breath exercise for an introduction in helping your child recognize the movement of breath in his body.

To begin, we simply count each inhale and exhale. For example, the first breath in is counted as 1, then the exhale is counted as 2 and so on, until we reach the number 10. Complete a few "practice" inhales and exhales prior to counting actual breaths.

When he is ready, tell your child to sit up straight, but comfortably, with his hands on his belly. Have him place his hands on his belly so that he is able to physically feel the breath entering and leaving his body as you count. Tell him to breathe in deeeeeeeeply (inhale), then to let it gooooooo (exhale). Count 1 for the inhale and 2 for the exhale.

Continue this way for five breath cycles, reaching a total count of ten. If your child is engaged and reacting positively, repeat the exercise again.

After the first few trials, try intervening less and less. For example, maybe he guides the inhale and exhale on his own, and you simply count his breaths, or perhaps you simply tell him to open his eyes after he completes counting to ten independently.

When done, ask your child if it was easy. No? Why does he think it wasn't easy? Ask him how it felt and if he noticed thoughts or feelings during the session. Ask him if he thinks it could be helpful to learn to pay attention to what he wants to focus on, not just whatever happens to come to mind.

With older kids and teens you can count a full breath cycle instead (following one in-breath and one out-breath all the way). This way, counting to ten would amount to ten in-breaths and ten out-breaths.

Nothing to do

Purpose: Body awareness, Mindfulness of breath, Focus, Calm

Best for: Ages 6+, groups or one-on-one

What you need: Nothing, A clock is optional

To begin, tell your child how busy your lives can be. Has he noticed how busy the last few weeks have been—with chores, school, moms' and dads' job and so on? How both of you are constantly supposed to do something—or that it might feel like that at times?

Next, tell him that for the following minute he can let go of all that. There's absolutely nothing to do but, of course to, breathe. To make the time fly he can simply focus on his breath. Try it out together.

Guided script:
Breathe in, breathe out.

There's nothing at all you have to do right now but this.

Breathe in and breathe out. At your own pace.

When ready, ask him how it felt to let go of the busyness.

7 and up

River of thoughts

Purpose: Body awareness, Mindfulness of breath, Recognizing Thoughts, Focus, Calm

Best for: Ages 7+, groups or one-on-one

What you need: Nothing

To do this activity, your child needs to have tried mindful breathing before. Try one of the other mindful breathing activities first and then come back to this one.

Paying attention to our breath helps us recognize thoughts and emotions for what they are. In this way, mindfulness helps us to deal with difficult thoughts – we have a choice to respond rather than to react. When we recognize our thoughts and emotions for what they are, we are less easily driven by them. This mindfulness activity helps us observe our thoughts and emotions so that it becomes more natural to us to do this even during difficult experiences.

Begin by guiding your child to breathe mindfully.

Do mindful breathing for two minutes while guiding him to pay attention to his thoughts.

Ask him to notice if thoughts happen. Tell him that thoughts are often self-talk, memories, fantasies, and plans. That there's nothing wrong in thinking, and that we are not trying to stop thoughts.

Tell him that he can imagine that his thoughts are floating down a stream – like leaves. That he can picture himself sitting beside a river. That he can watch thoughts pass by as they come and then focus on his breath again, instead of engaging with the thoughts – instead of continuing the thought on purpose.

For example, if a thought floats by saying: "Oh, I have soccer practice tonight," he can leave it be instead of planning what he needs to do before practice or fantasizing what he will do during practice.

Tell him that sometimes we accidentally grab or continue a thought and forget to pay attention to the breath, but that during this activity we learn to let thoughts go – we simply let them float downriver. We practice not automatically grasping or continuing every thought.

When ready, ask if he noticed thoughts. Did he grab any thoughts? It's okay if he did. What kind of thoughts did he grab? Did he notice any emotions that came with the thoughts? Were they happy, sad or stressful?

Anchor words

Purpose: Body awareness, Mindfulness of breath, Recognizing thoughts, Focus, Calm

Best for: Ages 7+, groups or one-on-one

What you need: Nothing

Anchor words give us some additional help to keep our attention on our breathing. It requires some simple preparation with your child to use these reminder words during a mindful breathing exercise, but after she understands how they work, she'll be able to use them easily on her own.

To start, have a conversation about what happens when her mind wanders. How does she bring her attention back to what she was doing? Explain to your child that sometimes, just one little word can keep her mind from wandering. We call these words anchor words, because they help our mind stay put the way an anchor helps a boat to stay in place.

Ask her to close her eyes and breathe in. As she breathes in, say the word "in," and tell her that is her first anchor word.

As she breathes out, say the word "out," and tell her that is her second anchor word. If there are other words she'd rather use, encourage her to do what makes her feel comfortable and stay engaged, but the words "in" and "out" are great starter words.

Continue to say the words while she takes fives breaths.

When she opens her eyes, ask her how it felt. Is she ready to breathe and think about the words "in" and "out" on her own? The idea is to say the words silently with each breath. She can then repeat the activity as many times as she likes.

When ready, ask your child how it felt and what she noticed during the session. Did she notice thoughts? Was it easier to pay attention to the breath while saying "in, out?"

Take note that this exercise can also be easily applied in real-life scenarios. For example, if test taking makes your child nervous, ask her to try five mindful breaths right before she begins the test. Similarly, if she gets stuck on a difficult test question, she could try five more and see if that makes it easier to focus. The use of anchor words can make it easier to complete a few mindful breaths when we are overwhelmed.

12 and up

Time machine
Purpose: Body awareness, Mindfulness of breath, Recognizing thoughts, Focus, Calm

Best for: Ages 12+, groups or one-on-one

What you need: Nothing

You will learn to recognize and label thoughts. This activity will demonstrate how our minds work. Your kid will learn that his mind may spend a lot of time in the future and the past. To do this activity, your kid needs to have tried mindful breathing before.

Our minds wander, and it's normal. We worry about the future and have a hard time letting go of regrets. Explain to your kid that at school, during class, his mind can easily wander to what he plans to do that evening. When this happens, his mind is preoccupied with the future—planning or imagining what it will be like. We could say that his mind is in the future.

Continue to explain that during soccer practice his mind might dwell on what a friend said at school. When this happens, his mind is preoccupied with the past—remembering what happened. We could say that his mind is in the past.

Sometimes our minds focus on what is happening right now and we can call that present-mindedness. When we are focused on the now, like this, we can do better because we are focusing on whatever it is we want to get done—instead of plans and worries.

Tell your kid that you will breathe mindfully for two minutes and see where their mind takes them—to the future, the past or somewhere else.

To start with, guide your child to breathe mindfully. Do mindful breathing for two minutes while guiding him to pay attention to his thoughts.

Ask him to notice if thoughts happen, and what quality the thoughts have.

Are his thoughts about planning or imagining future events?

Are his thoughts taking him back in time to something that happened?

Can he re-focus on his breath when his mind starts to wander?

Where are his thoughts when he pays attention to his breath?

After the exercise, ask him where his thoughts took him. Was he able to come back to the present moment by paying attention to his breath?

Counting to five and back

Purpose: Body awareness, Mindfulness of breath, Focus, Calm

Best for: Ages 12+, groups or one-on-one

What you need: Nothing

This is an elaborate breath counting exercise, so be sure to introduce mindful breathing before you try this one. Try it for a minute or two the first time.

Guided script:
Close your eyes gently and find your breath by breathing in deeply and then letting your breath out.

Taking another deep breath, and letting it out.

Now allow your breathing to just be normal; you don't need to alter it.

Begin to count each breath on the in-breath.

Start with 1 and count up to 5 and then backwards to 1 again.

Like this. 1 2 3 4 5 4 3 2 1 and on like this.

Counting up to 5, back down to 1, and up again.

This way, counting will focus attention on your breath and signal if you get lost counting. If we find ourselves at 8 or we don't remember what the last number was, we can just begin again at 1.

When you notice that your attention has drifted off and your mind is caught up in thoughts or feelings, gently bring the attention back to your breathing. Come back to the breath and begin again, starting with 1.

Each time you get distracted or find yourself on automatic pilot, come back to the breath and begin counting again with 1.

Well done. You can now open your eyes.

Labeling thoughts
Purpose: Body awareness, Mindfulness of breath, Recognizing thoughts, Focus, Calm

Best for: Ages 15+, groups or one-on-one

What you need: Nothing

This activity builds on the Anchor Words activity and helps us recognize the types of thoughts and experiences we encounter. Labeling can also further help to diminish the power of the thoughts and emotions we experience. Again, the idea isn't to stop your mind from generating thoughts, because that's close to impossible, but rather to notice where your mind goes and the quality of the thoughts that arise, and then gently bring your attention back to the breath.

To begin, ask your kid to come up with an anchor word to use when her mind wanders away from "in" and "out" – perhaps "thoughts" or "thinking" might work, for example – and to use that word in that moment, and then bring her attention back to her breath and the words "in" and "out."

Guide your kid to breathe mindfully.

Ask her to close her eyes and breathe in. As she breathes in, say the word "in," and tell her that is her first anchor word.

As she breathes out, say the word "out," and tell her that is her second anchor word. If there are other words she'd rather use, encourage her to do what makes her feel comfortable and stay engaged, but the words "in" and "out" are great starter words. Continue to say the words while she takes fives breaths. Then allow her to continue on her own.

Tell her that as thoughts arise, she can use a new anchor word, "Thinking," or that she can give it a label. The label may be "planning" or "remembering." It may be "worrying" or "judging" or "fantasizing." Ask her to create a label for the thought and then return to the breath.

Remind her that each time a thought arises, she can give it a label and let it go, bringing her attention back to the breath.

If, at any point, she finds herself thinking too much about what label to give, she can simply think, "Thinking, thinking..." and return again to the breath.

Let her breathe like this for a few minutes and then ask her how it was. Was she able to notice thoughts and label them? What kind of thoughts did she encounter and what kind of labels did she give them?

Whatever labels you want to give your thoughts is fine. The object is simply to become increasingly aware of what is happening in your mind and how thinking can take you out of the present moment.

CHAPTER 5

ACTIVITIES FOR JOY, GRATITUDE, AND KINDNESS

Gratitude Practice

You already know what gratitude is, and you've experienced gratitude many times, I'm sure, but here's one way of describing it:

Gratitude is a feeling of happiness that comes from appreciating something.

We can feel grateful for the good things in our lives, like

snuggling with a pet...

riding a bike...

feeling the sun on your face...

marveling at the moon...

observing a good quality in your child...

your favorite song...

your favorite food...

and for having a friend.

Sometimes we forget about the good stuff in our lives, especially when we're overwhelmed, upset, and stressed. But gratitude practice helps us to see the good. A friend told me that gratitude is like a flashlight that shows us all the good stuff we already have – the stuff we forget and the good we normally consider too small to feel happy about.

When scientists studied what makes people happy, they actually found that gratitude is one major thing that has the power to make us happy. The best part is that it's a skill. That's right, gratitude is a skill! And you can learn to feel good more often. You can learn to feel more joy for both big and small everyday things. And you know what? Joy is a building block for happiness!

Gratitude has the power to make you feel good—and you don't even have to wait for good things to happen to you. You can simply think about the good things you already have. You close your eyes (if you want to) and think about things you are grateful for (things that make you happy)—for a minute or so. It's this is easy to experience more joy, and it's a fun way to boost happiness together with your kids.

What are children grateful for? Here are some examples:
- Hugging mommy (That's what Anton says every day)
- Hugs and kisses
- Snuggling my cat
- Eating ice cream
- Having a friend
- That my bike tire isn't broken anymore
- Playing football

- The blueberry pie
- A new toy

Often times children think of material things and that's okay. But what's great is that we can help children discover gratitude for immaterial things that are always there for us.

More ideas of things to be grateful for:

- Family
- Friends
- A quality about yourself
- A talent
- Something nice that happened
- Something in nature
- Something you love to do
- Something you love to eat
- Something you've learned this year

Gratitude can be about anything, really. The roof over your head. Family. Your senses. The beauty of an evening sky. The birdsong you heard today. The scent of flowers. The warmth you feel inside your thick sweater. The sun on your face.

Let me share a short story called The Power of Gratitude:

A friend of mine told me how she used gratitude practice to help herself and her kids to cope with divorce. The divorce was obviously hard for everyone. Gratitude practice helped her and her kids balance their lives during a period of huge change. The practice let them see that there was a lot of good in life despite all the difficulty.

My friend noticed how a daily gratitude practice made her sons more focused on the positive things in life—happier. The practice helped them to think about the good more often, to balance the scale at a time when the scale would have easily tipped in favor of the negative.

She still remembers how happy she was listening to her boys and how much warmth she felt when her youngest boy shared how he was thankful for having a mom and a dad and his brothers—despite everything that was going on.

This is what you can learn through practice:
1. You can learn to be grateful for what you already have.
2. You can learn to appreciate the small things in life.
3. You can become better at feeling good.
4. You can learn that happiness comes from within.
5. You can discover a new, joyful way to connect with your kids.

WARNING!

BE SURE NOT TO MISS SOME OF THE BEST ACTIVITIES.

Please don't let the age recommendations restrict you.

The age recommendations are more about how difficult the exercises are than what age they are most suited for. So, for example, "3 and up" activities work fine for a teen or a grown-up, but "12 and up" activities are most likely too advanced for children under the age of six. "3 and up" activities are often great for older kids, teens, and even grown-ups. And you might want to start with some of them to introduce mindfulness in a super-easy way regardless of age.

3 and up

Bedtime thank you's – gratitude practice
Purpose: Gratitude, Positivity, Connection

Best for: Ages 3+, one-on-one

What you need: Nothing

This is a fun exercise to do with your child. Each night, before you fall asleep, think of all of the happy things that happened to you that day. Things you can be thankful for. Like a smile you got from a friend, meeting funny Auntie Sue, the yummy bananas you ate, or the time with your pet. Say them out loud, or write them in a journal, draw a picture of them, or whisper them to your heart, and see the things surrounding you. Make this a routine that helps you fall asleep with love and gratitude for your life.

Naturally, you can do this exercise any time of the day for a heartwarming experience. To help your child put it into practice, ask him to recall three things he is thankful for the next time he is sad or angry. Try this after you are both comfortable with gratitude practice. Ask him to notice how thinking about those things makes him feel. Are those thoughts comforting? He will likely say yes.

Make a joy list
Purpose: Positivity, Gratitude, Connection

Best for: Ages 3+, groups or one-on-one

What you need: Paper and pen

Together with your kid, make a list of things that make you smile. Thinking of things that make you smile, like people you love, silly stuff that happened, funny pets and movies, helps you feel better right on the spot. Pay attention to how that makes you feel inside when you prepare the list. Visit the list occasionally, and see if it makes you smile. Smiling can help calm down the stress response and releases feel-good hormones. See if you can do more of these joyful things daily.

Thank your child
Purpose: Gratitude, Positivity, Connection

Best for: Ages 3+, groups or one-on-one

What you need: Nothing

This seems almost too simple, but it's easy to forget that children often need to be taught to express gratitude. The easiest way is to model it yourself. Gratitude can be a hard concept to grasp at first. Thank your child often and explain why you thank him. Thank him for both big and small things. Thank him for opening the door or for saying something kind, or say how thankful you are for having him. Your motivation to do this will grow when you notice how your child starts to pay more attention to the things he is thankful for and how he's able to express his positivity more often. The more we pay attention to the things that make us happy – the happier we are.

Appreciate the good in people
Purpose: Gratitude, Positivity, Connection

Best for: Ages 3+, groups or one-on-one

What you need: Nothing

When you express your gratitude for friends and family, you help kids learn to appreciated the good in people. For example:

"I'm grateful for what Caroline did on the playground. She was so kind to you. She really tried hard to help you—by explaining to you that it's okay even when it's hard to climb the climber thingy. She was helping you understand that it takes time to get to be as good as she is. And that you shouldn't feel bad when you can't instantly do the same as she can. That was really kind of her."

Sharing gratitude
Purpose: Gratitude, Positivity, Connection, Understanding

emotions

Best for: Ages 3+, groups or one-on-one

What you need: A ball (optional)

This is a fun exercise to do with your child one-on-one or sitting in a ring with a group of kids. Each participant is to tell what they are thankful for. When you play this game one-on-one with your kid, you can sit opposite each other on the floor.

1. First, ask your child to listen and to pay attention to how it makes her feel inside when she plays this game.
2. Take the ball in your hand and say out aloud something that you are grateful for. For example, "I'm grateful for the delicious food we ate," or "I'm grateful for having time to play with you." "I'm grateful for the smile I got from Dad." "I'm grateful for the sunny weather and the warmth of the sun on my face."
3. Then, roll or throw the ball to your child and ask her to think of something she's grateful for and to share it with you. Give her some time to pay attention to her feelings.

Do a few rounds and together ask her to repeat it once more with her eyes closed, imagining being surrounded by whatever she's thankful for. Ask her to really pay attention to how it feels inside when she does that. When ready, discuss what kind of feelings you felt and if you were able to feel them somewhere in your bodies.

Gratitude tree

Purpose: Gratitude, Positivity, Connection

Best for: Ages 3+, groups or one-on-one

What you need: Colored paper to cut out leaves (double sided is nice for colorful leaves)

String or ribbon to hang the leaves on the tree branches

Scissors

Twigs or branches

Rocks to add stability to the tree

Vase

Grateful hearts

The Gratitude Tree activity is a fun way to count our blessings. The project is pretty simple and lots of fun. Spending time with your child talking about gratitude is a great way to spend Thanksgiving or a rainy day. It might even become a fun tradition for you.

Directions
1. Make a leaf cut out (or a few for variety) to use as your template. Trace the rest of the leaves on a bigger sheet, and cut them out.
2. Punch a hole at the top of each leaf and loop a piece of string through each.
3. Put stones in a vase and stand the tree branch among them.
4. Have your child draw or write about things he is grateful for on the leaves. If he is too young, you can write for him. You could also find some old photos and make a visual tree instead of writing things down.
5. You can make a few leaves of your own to model the concept for your child.
6. Hang the leaves from the branches.

Gratitude flowers
Purpose: Gratitude, Positivity, Connection

Best for: Ages 3+, groups or one-on-one

What you need: Colored paper to cut out flower parts, Glue, Scissors, Grateful hearts

This activity is similar to The Gratitude Tree, but instead of trees, you will do super-simple flowers.

Directions

1. Find fun colored paper for your gratitude flowers.
2. Start by cutting out a circle for the centre of the flower and write your name (or your child's name on it). Make it big enough so that you have ample space to write.
3. Next cut out big petals for the flower. Be creative and experiment with colors. A template for the centres and petals will help a lot, especially if your child wants to do the cutting.
4. Write down or draw the things you are grateful for on the petals. If your child is old enough, he can write his own; if not, then you can help him with that. You can draw pictures, too.
5. Glue the petals to the flower centre and you have your first gratitude flower!

If you do this with a group of children, you can do a whole garden of flowers! You can even place the flowers on a wall for an awesome "indoor garden" to which you can return to get a gratitude boost.

Gratitude for food

Purpose: Gratitude, Positivity, Connection

Best for: Ages 3+, groups or one-on-one

What you need: A moment after or during a meal

We can be thankful for the wonderful taste sensations and for having food in the first place. You can also remind your kid that the food she is eating involves many people and hard work. Remind her of the farmer, the people working at the grocery store, and the people who work to prepare your food. You can even make a game of it and try to think of the complete chain of people who have helped you to get the food on your table—all the way from the farmer sowing the seeds to the cook preparing the food.

Gratitude bracelet
Purpose: Gratitude, Connection, Positivity

Best for: Ages 4+, groups or one-on-one

What you need: a bracelet (you can make your own) and beads

Gratitude bracelets remind you to count your blessings. Any kind of bracelet will do, and you can choose as many beads as you like and figure out something you are grateful for per bead. For a younger child you may want to choose 3-5 beads.

Depending on the age of your child, you can either make one for them or do the bracelet together from scratch. It's actually very meditative to string the beads too.With a younger child you can simply let them choose the beads and talk about what gratitude is while you make his bracelet.

Tell your child that the bracelet will remind them of all the things they are grateful for. When they notice the bracelet, they can remember what each bead stands for (something they have decided on) or simply spend some time thinking of the things they are grateful for.

Wonder board
Purpose: Gratitude, Positivity, Connection

Best for: Ages 4+, groups or one-on-one

What you need: Colorful pens and paper

This is a fun activity to cultivate curiosity and wonderment. Talk with your child about the things that fill you with wonder. Maybe a fire engine makes him go WOW. Maybe a horse, a sunset or a hamburger. Or maybe he goes WOW when he gets a hug from someone special, when he skateboards, or listens to his favorite song.

Talk about the things. Ask him how it felt when he experienced those things. Did it make him excited? How did it feel inside his body? Ask him how thinking about those things makes him feel *now.* How does it feel in his body? Does it make him tingly in his stomach or something else?

Next, make a big WOW (or a sun) in the middle of the paper with a pen. Make it shine like the sun or special in some way like a cartoon WOW. Then recall the things and moments your child finds amazing, and draw or write them down around the WOW word. You can even add photos to it. Spend some time savouring the amazing things in your lives.

When ready, place your new wonder board somewhere your child sees often, such as near the dinner table or within sight of his bed.

Gratitude gift
Purpose: Gratitude, Kindness, Connection

Best for: Ages 4+, groups or one-on-one

What you need: Writing/drawing materials or art supplies

This is a compassionate spin on the traditional thank you note; a thank you note generally thanks someone for something, but this activity is a great way for a child to show appreciation to someone for simply existing. Consider doing this activity every few weeks, or however often the child finds it fun. She likely will find it fun, because the recipient of the gratitude gift is almost guaranteed to be honored and touched.

To begin, have a conversation with your child about a person in her life who is currently important. It could be a teacher, a friend, a sibling, a neighbor... anyone, really. Ask her to think of a reason why she is grateful to have that person in her life, and encourage her to draw or write her feelings. She should have fun with the project, decorating the "gift" or writing in a way that she knows will make her "important person" laugh or smile.

Explain that it's a good idea to let the people whom she cares about know that she is thankful for their presence. As she works, continue to talk with her about what makes that person so fantastic. When she eventually presents her thank you note or drawing, she will certainly brighten someone else's day; if, for some reason, she decides not to present her gratitude gift, she still spent a great deal of time thinking positively about someone else.

Happiness scrapbook
Purpose: Gratitude, Connection, Positivity

Best for: Ages 5+, groups or one-on-one

What you need: Scrapbook, pens, photos ...

Happiness scrapbooking is a fun way to journal family history and to remind yourself of all the things you are grateful for. Start a happiness scrapbook together with your child to find out what he likes and to spend more time together on a positive note.

Typical memorabilia used for scrapbooking include photographs, printed media, and artwork. Google "scrapbooking" for loads of great ideas. You can keep the journal simple, too, by adding a phrase or a short story per page if you wish. Tell your child that he can visit his happiness scrapbook to feel good and to remind himself of all the good things you've experienced and what you are grateful for.

Gratitude jar

Purpose: Gratitude, Connection, Positivity

Best for: Ages 5+, groups or one-on-one

What you need: A jar, pieces of paper, a pen

Sit down together with your child and discuss the meaning of gratitude. List things you are grateful for and write those ideas on pieces of paper. If your child is old enough he can write his own; if not then you can help him with that. You can draw pictures too.

When ready, fill a jar with gratitude. You can start with just ten things and make a habit of adding a few more each week as a family. It's a wonderful habit and you can pause and read them all on Mondays to brighten up your week. Tell your child that she can visit the jar to remind herself of all the things she's thankful for.

A gratitude jar will become a wonderful treasure you can come back to for a happiness boost.

It's a lot of fun to look back at all the happiness—all the joy you've experienced. See also: Kindness Jar.

Express appreciative joy

Purpose: Appreciative joy, Gratitude, Connection

Best for: Ages 5+, groups or one-on-one

What you need: Nothing

Have you ever felt happy about something and told a friend about it, and that friend suddenly got really happy for you? Didn't it feel great to experience that shared joy? Often we get out of touch with joy because of our life circumstances. But we can learn to access joy more often by sharing it! Talk about it when good things happen to others. Be vocal about the good that happens to your family and friends. Share how it makes you feel, and ask the kids how talking and thinking about others' joy makes them feel.

Spot appreciative joy

Purpose: Appreciative joy, Gratitude, Connection

Best for: Ages 5+, groups or one-on-one

What you need: Nothing

Point it out when you see your kids taking joy in the happiness of others. For example, when your kids tell you excitedly about something cool that happened to their friends.

1. Notice when your kid is happy for someone else.
2. Ask them how they feel and if they're happy for someone else. Explain how cool it is that you can feel joy for others—for their happiness.
3. Later, remind them about it, and ask them how it makes them feel to recall the memory.

The cool thing is that if we feel like we're totally out of luck (which we never are of course – you know this from gratitude practice), but if we feel out of luck, we can still find a million things to be happy for... if we look outside of ourselves. If we take part in the joy of others.

The ABCs of gratitude

Purpose: Gratitude, Positivity, Connection

Best for: Ages 6+

What you need: Nothing

Do this exercise together with your child. In a seated position or lying down, with eyes closed, make your way through the alphabet. Beginning with the letter "a," think of something you are grateful for that begins with each letter of the alphabet. "I am grateful for Auntie Sue, for bananas, for our cats..." See if you can make it all the way to "z" with a light and grateful heart.

When ready, ask your child how it felt and what she noticed during the session. Was it calming? Did she feel happier afterwards?

Happy memories
Purpose: Savoring positive memories, Gratitude

Best for: Ages 6+, groups or one-on-one

What you need: Nothing

Recalling fun events can make us smile and even laugh out loud. Just like we enjoy a yummy dessert, we can take delight in a memory of an experience.

You can use the following guided script with your child, or you can adapt it to be more suitable for your child's situation.

Guided script:
Sit or lie down.

Try to be really still.

Close your eyes gently.

Now remember a happy memory. Remember a time when you felt happy, something nice or fun that happened to you. Maybe

149

someone was kind to you. Perhaps you got a smile from a friend or your pet was happy to see you. Remember a wonderful moment like that. Simply close your eyes and bring it into your mind. Maybe you can even see the situation with your eyes closed. Like a dream.

Bring all your attention to your happy experience. Imagine the place and the people there. What did you see? Remember what you heard. Did something smell or taste good? See if you can remember more. Did someone make you smile? Who was it? Did you laugh?"

Notice what's happening inside you. How do you feel?

How does it feel in your body? Does it make you feel good?

If so, then let this feeling completely fill you so you know what it feels like.

You can put a smile on your face, if this makes you feel good. Even if it feels silly at first.

Silly is good. If you wish, let your smile grow and expand from you lips to your eyes.

How does your face feel? How does your body feel?

When ready, talk about the experience. How did recalling happy memories make him feel? Could he use this exercise on his own sometime?

7 and up

Daily gratitude
Purpose: Gratitude, Positivity, Reflection

Best for: Ages 7+, groups or one-on-one

What you need: A small dry-erase board, chalkboard, or a piece of paper and a pen

Help your child show gratitude regularly by incorporating this activity into his daily routine. It's best to practice this exercise in the evening when he has had a full day of experiences to reflect upon. Most importantly, don't turn this routine into a chore; it should be fun.

Prior to starting the daily gratitude routine, consider working with the child to decorate the dry erase board or chalkboard on which he'll share his gratitude sentences. This will help him feel involved in the exercise from the very beginning. Hang the board somewhere accessible: in the child's bedroom, on his door, or on the refrigerator. You can do this with a piece of paper too, simply use a magnet to attach the paper to the refrigerator.

Next, have a conversation about gratitude. Model by sharing something you're grateful for, and explain why you have gratitude for that particular thing. Stress the importance of showing gratitude for non-material items by modeling your gratitude for another person, opportunity or experience. Write your gratitude sentence on the dry erase board. After you've shown him what to do, tell your child it's his turn. If he needs assistance writing, help by giving him a sentence starter. For example, you can write something such as, "Today, I'm grateful for _____" and have him fill in the blank. Leave his gratitude sentence up until the next day, when he will create a new one.

To make this exercise even more practical, you can try it without a chalkboard. Simply ask your child to verbally list five things he is thankful for, and tell him to spend a minute thinking about each item on his list. This exercise can be used to help him calm down on his own, too.

Gratitude journal

Purpose: Gratitude, Positivity, Reflection, Connection

Best for: Ages 7+, one-on-one

What you need: A notebook and pen

Try this out yourself for a few days and then explain it to your kid. It's simple and fun. And great for teens. Keep a gratitude journal. It can be filled with text or pictures, whatever is most appropriate. It can be written in any type of book or notepad or on an electronic device. Anything that works for you will do. Try to add five things you are grateful for each day.

You might feel that doing this activity before you start your day works best. This might be a great way to end your day, or you might include it as a lunchtime activity. Do what feels best, and be grateful for all this life brings to you. One fun way of doing this is to write the journal before bed and read it in the morning for a great start to the day.

Gratitude photo challenge

Purpose: Gratitude, Connection, Positivity

Best for: Ages 7+, groups or one-on-one

What you need: A camera

If your child is old enough to handle a camera or a camera phone, challenge him to spend a week taking photos of things he is grateful for. Any camera will work.

Start by explaining what gratitude is and make list of things you both are grateful for to help your kid understand the concept. Then review the list for some potential themes to explore throughout the week—perhaps one theme per day.

152

Themes for a full week could look like this:

Monday: friends and family

Tuesday: food

Wednesday: nature

Thursday: music

Friday: beauty

Saturday: toys and tech

Sunday: comfort

You can follow up each day after dinner and spend some time sharing your photos and talking about the good stuff.

After the seven-day period, get together and share your photos and talk about them in detail. Ask your kid if he's been a bit happier that week focusing on the good. It is likely he will say yes.

Finally, print the photos and make a gratitude album or a fun board your kid can place somewhere he sees often.

To include more friends and family in the activity, you can upload the photos online—for example, to Instagram if you are both into that (and old enough). You may want to challenge your Facebook friends, too.

If you both enjoy the challenge, repeat it once or twice a year, adding to your gratitude album each time. It's a lot of fun to revisit the album, especially if you keep adding to it.

12 and up

Gratitude buddy
Purpose: Gratitude, Connection, Appreciative joy

Best for: Ages 12+, groups or one-on-one

What you need: A friend

Pick a friend and share the good with each other. You can start with your kid and later ask him or her to pick a friend to continue the practice with. Every day, or at least once a week, write or call or instant message what you are grateful for. This is a fun way to build your gratitude muscles. The fun thing is that you will feel joy for the good things your gratitude buddy experiences, too. You get to recall your own joys AND you get to feel appreciative joy for your buddy. It's a positive spiral!

This is a fun activity for a whole class at school. You could do this for a week or even a whole month, depending on how often you ask the kids to keep reporting to each other.

Gratitude stones
Purpose: Gratitude, Connection, Positivity

Best for: Ages 12+, groups or one-on-one

What you need: Nice smooth stones, a pen or hand paint

Pick stones that are round and smooth. Stones that feel nice to hold and have room for a word or two. Talk about gratitude together with your kid and list the things you are grateful for. Paint words or pictures together on the stones. You can go for elaborate artistic designs with patterns or simply paint a word per stone: joy, love, mommy, my pet, summer, kiss, a name of friend etc. You can paint your cat or the sun. The possibilities are limitless!

Google "hand painted rocks" for ideas. When you are done you can put the stones in a jar to make a gratitude jar or place stones around your home to remind you of the things you are grateful for.

Notice more joy

Purpose: Noticing emotions, Positivity, Gratitude

Best for: Ages 12+, groups or one-on-one

What you need: Nothing

Do this yourself for a few days and then explain to your kid how they can do it. When you experience joy during the next day, LET YOURSELF FEEL IT. Don't skip over it. It does not have to be intense joy; joy can be subtle and simple. Collect happy memories this way. Enjoy them as they happen and file them under joy. With practice, you will start to see what really matters in your life.

Notice appreciative joy

Purpose: Noticing emotions, Positivity, Gratitude

Best for: Ages 12+, groups or one-on-one

What you need: Nothing

This activity is almost identical to the previous one. The difference is that with this activity you can learn to discern and boost appreciative joy. Appreciative joy is about thinking of the good fortune of a loved one or a friend... or even a stranger. You feel joy at the good fortune of another person.

Do this activity yourself for a few days and then explain to your kid how they can do it.

When you experience joy for others during the next week, LET YOURSELF FEEL IT. Don't skip over it. It does not have to be intense joy; joy can be subtle and simple. Savor the feeling when your kids are joyful and when you meet friends who share something nice with you—whenever you see that someone has joy in their life. I'm sure you will find many opportunities. This can be as simple as checking in on Facebook, calling a friend, or meeting friends and asking them what's good in their lives right now. Collect happy memories this way. Enjoy them as they happen, and file them under appreciative joy.

Kindness Practice

Everyone wants to feel loved and cared for, right? It makes us feel good to receive kindness. How does it feel when someone says something kind to you? Yes, it makes you feel good. We like people who show us kindness. Shared kindness bonds us together. Kindness is a way to build new relationships and to strengthen existing ones.

Kindness is amazing. It even makes us feel good to see acts of kindness happen to someone else. Have you ever paid attention to how it feels when *you* say something kind—to a friend or a loved one or even a stranger? Yes, it, too, feels good. A simple kind thought has the power to make you feel good. Kind thoughts are rewarding for the thinker. You just wish for someone to be happy. You think it. Like this:

"I wish for my son to be happy."

"May you be happy, Anton."

"I wish for my mom to be happy."

"May you be happy."

And that's all! With some practice, you'll notice how thinking kind thoughts makes you feel. Hint: It makes you feel good. And that's the essence of the practice. When we think kind thoughts, we can experience feelings of kindness, calm, and happiness.

It gets easier with practice for us to experience these rewarding feelings. It gets easier to be kind, too. Kindness becomes more automatic.

When you practice kindness repeatedly, you teach your brain to experience kindness more often. This way, kindness is a skill that we can train ourselves in. I love kindness practice because it's so soothing, simple to do, and a heartwarming way to show love and care for each other.

This is what you can learn through practice:
1. You can learn empathy in a fun way.
2. You can learn that being kind makes you happy.
3. You can learn to appreciate kindness in others.
4. You can learn that happiness comes from within.
5. You can discover a new, heart-warming way to connect with your kids.

WARNING!

BE SURE NOT TO MISS SOME OF THE BEST ACTIVITIES.
Please don't let the age recommendations restrict you.

The age recommendations are more about how difficult the exercises are than what age they are most suited for. So, for example, "3 and up" activities work fine for a teen or a grown-up, but "12 and up" activities are most likely too advanced for children under the age of six. "3 and up" activities are often great for older kids, teens, and even grown-ups. And you might want to start with some of them to introduce mindfulness in a super-easy way regardless of age.

3 and up

Say more kind things
Purpose: Kindness, Positivity, Connection

Best for: Ages 3+, groups or one-on-one

What you need: Nothing

Be kind, especially when life feels hard—it's contagious. Show to your kids how kindness is contagious. Be super kind for a week! Simply say more kind things—even at times when expressing it feels redundant. See if your kids start doing the same, and ask them what made them do it.

Pass the kindness
Purpose: Kindness, Positivity, Connection, Understanding emotions

Best for: Ages 3+, groups or one-on-one

What you need: A ball (optional)

This is a fun exercise to do with your child one-on-one or sitting in a ring with a group of kids. Each participant will say something nice to the next kid. When you play this game one-on-one with your kid, you can sit across from each other on the floor.

1. First ask your child to listen and pay attention to how it makes her feel inside as you say nice things to her. Take the ball in your hand, look her in the eyes and say something nice.

For example:

"I like your smile."

"It's so much fun to play with you."

"I wish you to be happy."

"I wish you to be healthy and strong."

Give her some time to pay attention to her feelings.

2. Then, roll or throw the ball to your child and ask her to say something nice back to you (or another kid). Ask her to pay attention to how it makes her feel inside saying it.

Do a few rounds of this and discuss what kind of feelings you felt and if you were able to feel them somewhere in your bodies.

You can alter the "game" by closing your eyes when you send kind wishes to see if it's easier to feel that way. Then try sending kind wishes to friends and loved ones that are elsewhere. See how it makes you feel.

A great way to end the activity is to send kind wishes to yourself.

For example:
"May I be happy."

"May I be healthy and strong."

Kind memories
Purpose: Kindness, Understanding Emotions, Emotional Intelligence

Best for: Ages 3+, groups or one-on-one

What you need: Somewhere to lie down comfortably

This activity will help your child connect with kind thoughts and set kind intentions.

Guided script:
Lie down so that you are comfortable.

Close your eyes.

Now, remember a time when someone was kind to you. Remember what it was like. Remember what happened.

Remember how it made you feel. Maybe you felt it in your body. Maybe it made you smile. Maybe you even laughed out loud.

Now, remember when you did something kind to someone. Maybe you helped a friend or mom and dad. How did it feel to be kind to someone? Maybe you felt it in your body?

Would you like to do something kind to someone today? How do you think it will make them feel? How do imagine it will make you feel?

Wish on a star

Purpose: Kindness, Positivity, Connection

Best for: Ages 3+, groups or one-on-one

What you need: Nothing

The last few days, we have been looking out for shooting stars ... with no luck. Yesterday, Anton pretended to see a falling star and insisted that he could make a wish. I said he could and he wished that daddy would come to sleep with him when he went to bed instead of doing grown-up stuff. It was so sweet that I came up with this simple variation on loving kindness practice that I call "Wish On a Star."

Essentially, you look up at the sky, and you pretend to see a falling star. Or you wish on a star that's there. Any star will do ... even a pretend one :-) Then you get to make two wishes:

1. One for yourself
2. And one for somebody you care for.

Finally, you pay attention to how it feels to wish these kind things for yourself and others.

To sum it up ... it goes like this:

1. You look up at the sky (or out of the window) and pretend to see a falling star. You can do this in bed, too, by simply pretending that you can see a starry night sky.
2. Then you get to make two wishes: one for yourself and one for somebody you care for. As a parent or educator, you can start and set the tone. Instead of wishing yourself a Tesla, you could find something more heartfelt and kind to demonstrate to the kids.

Here are some examples:

I wish for you to be healthy.

I wish for Grams to be happy.

I wish you a fun day.

I wish for myself to be healthy and happy.

Finally, you pay attention to how it feels to wish these kind things for yourself and others. You simply ask the kids how it feels to wish kind things.

Yesterday at dinner, Anton asked if we could play "Wish on a star" again. He had the sweetest, kindest wishes, and it made us all feel happy :-)

Loving-kindness bedtime wishes

Purpose: Kindness, Positivity, Connection

Ages: 4+, one-on-one

What you need: Nothing

This calm bedtime routine will help your child wind down and think about others in a loving and compassionate way. After she has been tucked into bed, tell her to think about one person to whom she'd like to send love. It could be someone she's thankful for, someone she loves, someone who had a bad day, a stranger she observed and wondered about, or a person she saw on the news. It can be anyone.

The words you (and she) will say should vary, based on her age. When first incorporating this exercise into the child's routine, it's best to model it for her by doing it yourself.

Here are some examples of phrases that she might use:
I send love to _____.

I send kindness to _____.

I send happy thoughts to _____.

May _____ be happy.

May _____ be healthy.

May _____ find peace.

May _____ let go of sadness.

Younger children may say this aloud, mimicking your model. As they get older, they may grow to take on this exercise as an independent and silent loving-kindness meditation. With a young child, you can even start with her plush toy: "May you be happy, [insert toy's name]."

Sending kind thoughts
Purpose: Kindness, Positivity, Connection

Best for: Ages 4+, groups or one-on-one

What you need: Somewhere to sit or lie down

Ask your child to sit down (or lie down) and close her eyes. Take a few deep breaths together and guide her through a short visualization.

Guided script:
Think of someone you love or like a lot. It could be mom or dad, grams or grandpa, even your pet if you want to.

You can imagine that person or pet standing in front of you, if you wish.

Think of something super nice to tell them.

It could be something like "I wish you to be happy" or "I wish you a fun day!".

Say the super nice thing quietly in your mind.

Say it once more with a smile if you wish.

Imagine how that makes the person or pet feel.

Maybe they smile back at you.

Maybe they say the same thing to you.

Notice how it makes you feel.

Now, say the same super nice thing (or something else nice) to yourself—quietly in your mind.

It could be something like "May I be happy" or "May I have a fun day!".

Notice how it makes you feel.

Open your eyes.

When ready, ask how this exercise made her feel. Would she like to do it again some time? Could it make her feel better when she's sad or worried?

Sending kind thoughts visualization

Purpose: Kindness, Positivity, Connection

Best for: Ages 5+, one-on-one

What you need: Nothing

We often focus on teaching children how to not make others feel bad, but how often do we spend time teaching them about spreading joy and gratitude to each other, to focus only on spreading the positive? This exercise will help your child become familiar with the feelings of saying positive things to someone that she cares about.

Ask your child to pick someone in her life whom she loves, someone who makes her smile. You can begin by talking with your child a little bit about this person. What is it about this person that makes her happy? What is special about this person? Keep in mind that children experience love without conditions, and their choice of person may surprise you. They might even choose a pet rather than a person. This is ok; they are sending loving, compassionate thoughts into the world, and this is always a positive thing.

Once your child has opened up about a person close to her heart, make sure she is comfortable. Have your child close her eyes and think about the person she loves. Have her bring her hands to her heart and hold them there, imagining that she is giving that person a warm, tight hug. Help your child picture this person. Maybe talk about what clothes they might be wearing, what they might smell like or any other sensory connection that will help make the image more real for your child. Here's an example of how you can do it.

Guided script:
When you close your eyes, imagine (for example) Grandma's face. Think about how happy it makes her feel when you hold her close to your heart and hug her. Imagine the smile on her face. She is happy and laughing.

Now, I want you to imagine Grandma doing something that you know she loves. It is ok if you need a few minutes to think about this. Just take your time and let me know when you are ready.

Have your child give you an idea of what they are imaging. It can be a simple one or two word description. If, for instance, Grandma is in her garden, you can then help your child build the picture with a little guided visualization.

Grandma is in her garden, the sun is warm, and there is a beautiful butterfly on one of her flowers. She is smiling, her body is strong and healthy, she is relaxed and happy.

I want you to imagine walking up to Grandma, giving her a big hug, and sending her kind and loving thoughts. When you send kind and loving thoughts, you begin by filling your own heart up with love, so much love that it almost feels like you might burst. Now take all of that love in your heart and send it out, as a gift to Grandma.

If your child is old enough to truly understand the intent, you can have her make kind and compassionate statements such as "May you be happy, healthy, and strong" or "May you be happy and peaceful" as a way of closing the exercise.

After a few moments of quiet, ask your child how it felt to send kind thoughts to that person. Often, a child will comment that she feels happy, calm, relaxed, and wonderful. If there is a strong feeling of happiness, point out that it only took a short time for her to achieve that feeling.

Then, tell her that she is going to continue by sending kind thoughts to herself. For a younger child, begin by trying a self-hug. For that, tell her to use both hands: she should wrap both arms gently around herself for a good self-hug.

Tell her to close her eyes and send those same thoughts she sent to the other person to herself, feeling the same love and kindness that she shared with someone else: "May I be happy, healthy, and strong" or "May I be happy and peaceful."

When ready, ask your child how it felt and what she noticed during the session. How does she feel about herself after doing this practice? How does she feel about the person she sent kind thoughts to?

I hope you get the warm fuzzies, like I often do with this exercise. If you don't, no problem; try it a few times to get used to sending and receiving kind thoughts.

Happy wake-up ritual
Purpose: Kindness, Positivity, Connection

Best for: Ages 5+, one-on-one

What you need: Nothing

Many families have mindful bedtime rituals, but the morning is also a fantastic time to incorporate mindfulness into a child's daily routine. One great way to help your child start the day off on a positive, compassionate note is to encourage her to determine a specific kind intention. Instead of having an intention to "do well in school" or "play soccer at recess," help her set a goal to do something positive for someone else. It could be as simple as calling grandma after school, sharing a toy with a friend, or smiling and saying hello to a sibling when he or she enters the room. Consider sharing your own kind intention with your child each morning as an example.

It may help to focus on the effect the intention may have on both the child and the recipient of the kind intention. For example, if the child intends to call her grandmother, you could ask, "What do you think she will say?"

Later in the day, follow up with the child to find out, and if she didn't have an opportunity to carry out her kind intention, that's okay—simply let her know that there's always tomorrow.

Kindness jar
Purpose: Kindness, Connection, Positivity

Best for: Ages 5+, groups or one-on-one

What you need: A jar, pieces of paper, a pen

My son Anton figured this one out. We were playing with our Gratitude Jar, and he said that we could add some kind wishes to the jar. We did, and we still do. In other words, our gratitude jar became a gratitude *and* kindness jar :-) Why not do both? If you want to start a kindness jar or expand your gratitude jar, you can do the following.

Start by writing down your kind wishes on pieces of paper. You can start with just two things and make a habit of adding a few more each week as a family. It's that simple. My son likes it so much that he's usually the one to prompt us to write down a few kind wishes or things that have been good. It's a wonderful habit. See also: Gratitude Jar.

Help others
Purpose: Kindness, Compassion, Positivity, Connection

Best for ages 6+, groups or one-on-one

What you need: An opportunity to get involved

Getting your children involved in helping others, even in small ways, helps them to develop an awareness about themselves that extends further than just their immediate needs, wants, and feelings. Compassion is a big part of mindfulness, and it is also a concept that must be demonstrated, practiced, and learned.

Our lives today are incredibly busy, so much so that the idea of trying to squeeze in more time to become "involved" seems impossible. What is important here is perspective and intention. Involvement in helping others does not need to be several hours a week devoted to a charity, although it can be. In this case, it is more about helping your child recognize the little ways in which they can be of service, share themselves, and become a part of their community.

Start with small things, like bringing the newspaper from someone's driveway up to their door, opening the door for someone, expressing kind thoughts to a sad friend, etc. These actions build upon each other and become contagious.

7 and up

What I like about me
Purpose: Self-kindness, Positivity

Best for: Ages 7+, groups or one-on-one

What you need: Writing materials (optional)

This exercise is so simple, yet so very powerful. Try it out yourself for a few days and then explain it to your child on her terms. You can keep a journal, notebook or pad of paper by your bedside if you wish. Each night, before you go to bed, list three things you liked about yourself that day. They can be simple things, like I let someone cut in at the traffic light.

They can be big things: I like that I am a patient person with my friends. There are no right or wrong things to put on your list; any three will do. Write them down, go to sleep, and read them over the next morning before you get out of bed. Gradually, this exercise can change the way you view yourself and how you interact with the world. As you compliment yourself, you can learn to more readily accept compliments from others because you have a base of love from which to respond. Give it a try and see how it feels.

Journaling kind wishes

Purpose: Self-kindness, Compassion, Reflection, Connection

Best for: Ages 7+, groups or one-on-one

What you need: A notebook and pen

Journaling can be a really nice way for a teen or an older kid to practice kindness—this way they can do it alone. They can take their time to send kind wishes and see how it makes them feel. You can help them get started with these simple kindness prompts:

Today I wish for myself...

Today I wish for a loved one...

Today I wish for someone I don't know that well...

Today I wish for a frenemy...

Today I wish for the whole world...

Connect
Purpose: Kindness, Compassion, Connection

Best for: Ages 7+, groups or one-on-one

What you need: Nothing

Explain to your kid that it's easy to spend time with the people you know. But today, she could try to come out of her comfort zone and connect with people she hasn't met or people she doesn't see very often. It's not complicated. Ask her to be kind and to say hi to a kid she hasn't spoken to before or ask "what's up?" of another kid she doesn't know that well. Ask her to see how it makes them both feel.

Loving-kindness towards self and others
Purpose: Kindness, Compassion, Positivity

Best for: Ages 10+, groups or one-on-one

What you need: Nothing

This activity takes the original Sending Kind Thoughts activity and expands it to include those people with whom we might have a less than positive relationship, along with people the world over whom we have never met. Some of our most challenging situations in life involve dealing with people and circumstances with which we are not familiar. This exercise will help an older kid learn the difficult skill of expressing compassion and understanding in difficult situations.

Begin by having your kid sit or lie down, relaxed and quiet, taking several deep breaths. You can use the following guided script with your kid, or you can adapt it to be more suitable for your child's situation.

Guided script:
I want you to imagine that you are sitting, facing another version of you. You are worthy of all the happiness and love in the world, and I want you to give this gift to yourself. Give yourself a big smile, maybe even a hug, and wish yourself happiness, joy, and love.

You can repeat after me: "May I be healthy and strong." "May I be happy." "May I be peaceful." Imagine yourself accepting it and bringing it into your heart.

Now, imagine that sitting next to you is someone that you love or care about a great deal. It can be any person, or you may even choose a pet. Smile at them, and picture some of the love in your heart spreading out and reaching towards them. Wish them love, joy, and happiness.

Let's continue sending that kindness together. You can repeat after me: "May you be healthy and strong." "May you be happy." "May you be peaceful."

Now, picture them accepting it and wishing these wonderful thoughts to you in return.

Now, sitting next to them, imagine someone whom you might not know so well. It might be someone you know from school, a kid down the block or a member of your team that you barely talk to.

Show this person the same kindness and compassion that you showed yourself and your loved one. Smile at them and share your love and compassion with them. You can repeat after me: "May you be healthy and strong." "May you be happy." "May you be peaceful."

Now imagine the person smiling back at you, wishing you happiness.

Now picture someone you don't particularly get along with well. It may be someone who is not very nice to people at school or maybe someone you had an argument with. Imagine them sitting in front of you and give them a big smile. We are all alike in the way that we all wish to be loved, safe, and happy. So, wish the person love, joy, and happiness. You can repeat after me: "May you be healthy and strong." "May you be happy." "May you be peaceful."

Now imagine the person smiling back at you, wishing you happiness.

If this feels hard to do, don't worry, it's okay. You don't have to do it; you can try later if you wish. And you can always return to a loved one, a family member, or a friend, for example. Simply imagine a loved one again.

Finally, picture all of the people in the world, the whole world. That's a lot of people. See them all spread out all over the world. So many happy faces. Give them a big smile and wish them all of the happiness, love, and joy there is in the world. You can repeat after me: "May we be healthy and strong." "May we be happy." "May we be peaceful."

Imagine all of them smiling and sending you kind thoughts of love, joy, and happiness. That's a lot of love!

When done, ask your child how he feels. How do you feel about yourself after doing this practice? How do you feel about those people you love? How about those people you have a more difficult relationship with? How do you feel about everyone in the world? What might you have in common with all those other people?"

If the exercise feels difficult, you can always skip the part with the more challenging people. If you're both new to loving-kindness practice, then it's likely best to start without the challenging person.

12 and up

Don't put yourself down
Purpose: Self-kindness, Mindful speech, Impulse control

Best for: Ages 12+, groups or one-on-one

What you need: Nothing

Try this one yourself and then explain the activity to your kid on her terms. Today, try to catch yourself the next time you belittle or criticise yourself (or somebody else). Instead, try to be constructive and kind. So, for example...

When you spill milk.

Say to yourself kindly: It's okay. It happens to everyone.

When you feel embarrassed.

Say to yourself kindly: It's okay, everyone feels like this at some point. And this feeling will pass.

When you feel that you have failed.

Say to yourself kindly: Don't worry. We'll fix this! We'll figure a way.

When you want to belittle or criticise someone else:

Pause and say something kind instead.

Remember, don't put yourself down, especially in front of the kids. Kids will copy your behavior.

Kindness boost

Purpose: Self-kindness, Compassion

Best for: Ages 12+, groups or one-on-one

What you need: Nothing

Try this one yourself and then explain the activity to your kid on her terms. Be kind to yourself, especially when life feels hard. Be kind towards yourself and see how it changes the game. This exercise works best when you've practiced sending kind thoughts for some time.

1. Be kind to yourself when you "fail". Send kind thoughts to yourself when life feels tough—when it feels like you are failing, and you are frustrated or angry. Send kind wishes to yourself (or another person if sending kind wishes to yourself feels though). See if it changes the situation.

Send kind wishes to yourself like this with your inner voice:

"May I be happy."

"May I be at ease."

2. Be kind when someone does something you don't like (e.g. your child misbehaves). Try sending kind wishes the next time this happens. You can do it with your inner voice secretly. See how it affects you.

Send kind wishes (to your child) with your inner voice:

"May you be happy."

"May you be at ease."

Or say with your inner voice:

"I Love You."

CHAPTER 6

ACTIVITIES FOR EMOTIONAL INTELLIGENCE AND REGULATION

Difficult emotions can be tough for anyone to deal with. Fear and anger can hit us unexpectedly, and without prior practice for dealing with these feelings, we can be thrown off balance and react badly. Mindfulness practice can help us create space between a strong emotion and our actions.

The following exercises can help you and the kids recognize emotions when they arise and provide techniques for working with them so they do not take over your lives.

Simply noticing and naming emotions can go a long way to helping manage them when they are more intense. With practice, we can learn to notice our emotions and accept them as they are. When we understand how emotions work and we are aware that we are, in fact, experiencing emotions, it allows us to pause, calm down, and reflect before we take action. We can respond in a more conscientious way, without getting hurt or hurting the feelings of others.

Learning to identify and express their feelings helps kids cope when they become overwhelmed. When they are aware of their inner life and are able to observe it, emotions and thoughts can lose their power over them, and they will be better equipped to respond rather than react.

As kids become more self-aware and better able to handle their emotions, they can eventually learn to handle those of other people. They can learn to recognize how others struggle with their emotions, too. This emotional intelligence helps guide their thinking and actions so that they make more skillful decisions and can attend to the feelings of others as well. Ultimately, they become more skillful both emotionally and socially.

The following activities help us recognize, understand, and navigate emotions. They will also help you to talk about emotions together with your kid.

If you have a young child, then "Trying out emotions" is a fun activity to get started with. Essentially, you role play and try to recall how major emotions feel. You try and see if you can feel them in your body. We had a blast trying this out with Anton when he was three. I was amazed at how many emotions my son could imitate. It wasn't a peaceful session by a long way, and it doesn't have to be. We laughed and exaggerated the emotions and made funny faces (happy, sad, disgusted, surprised, disappointed, and so on).

The following activities can help kids
1. Recognise emotions and thoughts for what they are.
2. Manage difficult emotions.
3. Reduce anxiety.
4. Understand that they have a choice… that sometimes you get to decide how you respond.
5. Become more skillful both emotionally and socially.

Let me share a short story called Grumpy Daddy:

Here's an example of how we can learn to manage feelings. This happened last summer. I was stressed and a little angry, too. I was tired and anxious about work stuff. And I just wanted some peace and quiet. After getting up at 5am and working eight hours straight, I had to hurry to go on a picnic with my parents-in-law. Stress was affecting the quality of my thoughts:

I looked at the sky and was sure it would rain...

(which it did not)

...the whole picnic felt like a bad idea...

(it turned out to be the opposite)

...and I simply didn't want to go.

My mind made all these excuses for not going—for not taking care of myself. My three-year-old son Anton noticed what was going on and asked me if I was sad. After some soul-searching, I took a deep breath and told him the truth. Yes, I was a little sad and a little angry at myself for not taking care of myself better that day. I wasn't sad because of him or because he wanted to go on the picnic. I had simply worked too much without a break, and I was a little overwhelmed. His response was sweet.

Anton: "Daddy, it's okay... We can go... and you can listen to the water."

Me: "What?!"

I was dumbfounded.

Anton continued: "You can listen to the water, and you will not be sad anymore."

He sounded like a sage from a seventies kung fu movie. And then it dawned on me. What he said and did made perfect sense! He had helped me acknowledge my mood and name it. Which I hadn't done by myself. I had been too busy being a grumpy daddy. I hadn't noticed how my mood was affecting my thoughts. Then he pulled the oldest trick in the (mindfulness) book. He asked me to focus on my senses to calm down. Bravo! Not bad for a three-year-old!

So, we went on the picnic, and we focused on our senses. We listened to the little stream running down to the beach...

to the waves...

the wind...

we paid close attention to flowers and ants...

we smelt the pine trees...

and tasted some awesome blueberries. I felt calm and recharged. It was the best day that week!

My little "guru" had helped me
1. notice, name and accept the state I was in
2. focus on my senses to calm down and recharge.

The cool thing is that when you admit to yourself that you are, in fact, sad, angry, stressed or anxious, it takes the edge off the emotion. This is something you can do with your kids, too. And on your own to de-stress. You can help your children notice and accept their emotional state before it escalates. When they are bored, annoyed or frustrated, for example. At the first signs. Before they go berserk.

Oftentimes, I simply ask my son to name the emotion he is experiencing, and it helps a little. When I notice that he is getting frustrated, I ask him to pause and express his feelings. After checking in on your kid's emotional state like this, you can continue by helping him or her pay attention to his or her senses. And when you are in a calm state you can talk about whatever it is that is causing the discomfort. We use these mindfulness "hacks" with my son all the time. He knows it works for him... and for grumpy daddy. Okay, let's try some activities!

WARNING!

BE SURE NOT TO MISS SOME OF THE BEST ACTIVITIES.

Please don't let the age recommendations restrict you.

The age recommendations are more about how difficult the exercises are than what age they are most suited for. So, for example, "3 and up" activities work fine for a teen or a grown-up, but "12 and up" activities are most likely too advanced for children under the age of six. "3 and up" activities are often great for older kids, teens, and even grown-ups. And you might want to start with some of them to introduce mindfulness in a super-easy way regardless of age.

3 and up

Cloudy or sunny

Purpose: Understanding emotions, Emotional intelligence

Best for: Ages 3+, groups or one-on-one

What you need: Somewhere to sit or lie down comfortably

This activity teaches your child to role-play and notice emotions in a fun way.

Guided script:
Lie down so that you are comfortable.

Now, close your eyes and pretend that you are out on a beautiful field. It's summer and it's warm and sunny. Maybe you can hear a bumblebee.

Look up to the sky and imagine that you are a cloud.

What kind of cloud are you? Are you white and fluffy—and floating gently in the breeze?

Are you dark grey, angry and about to burst?

Are you a rain cloud letting go of all the anger? If so, imagine letting your rain drops fall. Imagine cool water drops falling. Letting go of the weight.

Now let your angry raindrops fall away. Feel how you get lighter.

Now, if you want to, you can imagine that you are the sun—shiny, warm and happy.

When you are done, ask your child how it felt to play this game and how he is feeling now.

Calming Glitter Jar
Purpose: Emotional regulation, Focus, Calm

Best for: Ages 3+, groups or one-on-one

Materials:

- Small jar (make sure it will hold liquid without leaking)
- Clear glue
- Glitter (any colors you like)
- A few drops of food coloring
- Hot water
- Whisk or a stick

The Calming Glitter Jar is a proven mindfulness tool which can help to relax both kids and adults of all ages. Also, the Calming

Jar offers a practical way to "meditate" with a kid who doesn't want to sit still. You fill a jar with glitter, glue, and water, and your kid can use the jar after that to focus and calm down.

Visit my blog for pictures and videos:
www.blissfulkids.com/umab/

Directions

Warning: you may need to use your mindfulness skills to stay calm when your kid disperses glitter all over the place ;-)

This is a great tool for calming down, and it's simple to make. Depending on the sort of glue you use, you may have to experiment to get the consistency just right for you. That's part of the fun. You can experiment with about 20% glue, 80% water, and add as much glitter as you feel comfortable with. The more glue you use, the longer it will take for the glitter to settle after you have shaken the jar. You can use clear school glue and glitter, or glitter glue with added glitter to get the effect you want.

1. Pour glue and hot water (tap water is okay) into the jar and mix with a whisk. The glue makes the liquid thicker and makes impressive swirls of glitter.
2. Add some glitter. You can start with 1-2 tablespoons of glitter. I prefer to combine both chunky and finer glitter. For a pink jar, I used red hearts and purple, pink, and iridescent glitter. Iridescent glitter will give a nice, light look, so be sure to try it out.
3. Add a drop or two of food coloring to make it more exciting.
4. When everything is blended, put the lid on and give it a good shake so the glitter is dispersed throughout.
5. Then let it cool without the lid.
6. You can secure the lid with super glue.
7. Try it out together. Shake it!

When you've completed the jar with the glitter, you can explain the purpose of the jar. Shake it and tell your child that sometimes our minds are full of thoughts, swirling around like the glitter in the jar. Sometimes we experience angry thoughts. Sometimes sad thoughts.

Tell them that it's okay to have strong feelings but that we can calm those thoughts and our bodies as well. One way to do this is to let your thoughts settle like the glitter in the jar. When our minds are calm, it's easier to work out problems and to talk about whatever it is that is causing us to be upset. Shake the jar up until the glitter is spinning wildly. Then set it on a table or the floor and calmly watch it with your child until the glitter, and your minds, are all settled down.

That's it! The idea is that your child can learn to use the jar on his own when he's experiencing difficulty with emotions.

Balloon calm-down

Purpose: Emotional regulation, Focus, Calm

Best for: Ages 3+, groups or one-on-one

What you need: Nothing

This strategy is one to use in a difficult emotional moment. But be sure to introduce this exercise when your child is in a good mood. To begin, tell your child that she is going to blow up an imaginary balloon. Have her "hold" the balloon in the open palm of her hand, and ask her to identify the balloon's color to immediately engage her in the exercise.

Then, model the activity by putting your hand to your mouth and tell her to do the same. Talk her through the process of "blowing up the balloon." As she holds her hand to her mouth, she should keep blowing, blowing, blowing, until the balloon is as big as it can get. Tell her that with each blow, she's blowing out the thoughts of anger, frustration or sadness that were bothering her.

Once the imaginary balloon is as big as she thinks it can get, she can either pop it or tie it off and let it go.

When ready, ask her how it felt and what she noticed. Ask her if there's a difference in how she feels afterwards.

Play feelings charades
Purpose: Recognizing emotions, Emotional intelligence

Best for: Ages 3+, groups or one-on-one

What you need: Cut-outs from magazines, a bag or a hat

This is a fun game to play as a family. Find photos of faces depicting various feelings. You can use magazines or Google image search to print out expressive faces. Once you have your faces cut out and ready, put them in a bag or a hat and have each family member choose a card and act out the feeling, one by one. The other family members have to guess what feeling is being acted out. Children love to play this game and are always laughing hysterically by the end. Not only do they get to practice recognizing feelings in themselves but they also learn how to observe those feelings in others.

This activity was kindly inspired by my child and family therapist friend, Michelle Paget, who has a private practice that focuses on building social emotional skills for children and families with the help of yoga and mindfulness. For more information about Michelle, you can visit her website at www.michellepagettherapy.com.

Get artsy
Purpose: Mindfulness of emotions, Positive expression of emotions

Best for: Ages 4+, groups or one-on-one

What you need: Art materials of choice

This is a simple technique that appeals to all ages. Present your child with some art materials and help or encourage her to show how she is feeling through art. This might range from erratic scribbles for a young child to simple clay sculptures for an older child.

This activity supports mindfulness because it helps the child focus on something other than intense negative feelings and because making feelings into something tangible makes them more real. When something is real we can cope with it more effectively. Also, you might want to keep the child's art and show her the difference between art she made when she was upset and art she made when she was calm and mindful. Help her to see how she was able to move herself from one place to the next.

The quiet place
Purpose: Calm, Relaxation

Best for: Ages 3+, one-on-one

What you need: A space devoted to quiet, calm, and comfort

We all need a place to go where we can be alone with our thoughts, especially when we are upset or troubled. Children are no different. Have a designated area in your house that is a quiet place. Do not confuse this with a time out punishment place.

The quiet place can be an area created specifically for mindfulness or just a place where your child feels the most comfortable. If possible, fill the space with items that promote mindfulness. For example, add soft blankets and pillows if your child wants to sit or relax while she calms herself, or a music player with ear buds loaded with relaxing music or prerecorded meditative scripts. Fill the area with calming colors and textures and anything that your child has indicated brings her to a more peaceful, centered place. Make sure the quiet place has an open-door policy. No matter what is going on, let your child go to the quiet place if she needs to, without question.

Read a book with emotion
Purpose: Understanding emotions, Emotional intelligence

Best for: Ages 3+, one-on-one

What you need: A story book

Children may struggle to think of an example of when they experienced a specific feeling. Children struggle even more with the intense feelings of anger, fear, and sadness. Books are a wonderful resource to offer children examples of specific feelings and can normalize those feelings, as well.

Don't just read the book. Stop and ask your child questions along the way, like, "Annie sure does look angry. Can you think of a time when you were that angry? I sure got angry when..." This will help your child to make connections between the book's characters and his own feelings.

This activity was kindly inspired by my child and family therapist friend, Michelle Paget, who has a private practice that focuses on building social emotional skills for children and families with the help of yoga and mindfulness. For more information about Michelle, you can visit her website at www.michellepagettherapy.com.

Relaxation song
Purpose: Emotional regulation, Calm

Best for: Ages 4+, groups or one-on-one

What you need: Nothing

Similar to using a mantra, children can use simple childhood songs repeated calmly in their minds to help with relaxation. In a seated position with eyes closed, think of a simple song that you know the words to. "Row Your Boat" or "Twinkle, Twinkle, Little Star" are two easy songs to remember.

Have them sing the song silently in their head. Each time they sing the song through, have them touch a finger to their thumb, starting with the index finger and working through to the pinky finger. When they reach the pinky finger, they will have repeated the song through four times and will likely feel much calmer.

Mindfulness first aid kit

Purpose: Calm, Relaxation, Focus

Best for: Ages 4+, one-on-one

What you need: A small bag or container with child-specific calming and centering items

You will not always be at home when your child needs to practice mindfulness, and your child may not be at the point where all he needs to do is breathe and center his thoughts. For these cases, it is good to have a mindfulness kit. This can be just a small bag that contains age-appropriate mindfulness inducers, such as music, essential oils, sensory items or even a journal to write in or draw through their emotions.

Trying out emotions

Purpose: Understanding emotions, Emotional intelligence, Connection

Best for: Ages 4+, groups or one-on-one

What you need: Nothing

The idea is to see how it makes you feel inside when you hear words that describe emotions. This exercise is a simple form of role-play or visualization you can do with your child. When you read the words to your kid, spend at least ten seconds with each word. With older children, you can use subtler emotions. You can expand or contract the list of emotions depending on the age of your kid.

If you have a young child, then "Trying out emotions" is a fun activity to get started with.

Essentially, you role play and try to recall how major emotions feel. You try and see if you can feel them in your body. We had a blast trying this out with Anton when he was three. I was amazed at how many emotions my son could imitate. It wasn't a peaceful session by a long way, and it doesn't have to be. We laughed and exaggerated the emotions and made funny faces (happy, sad, disgusted, surprised, disappointed, and so on).

Guided script:
I am going to list different emotions. See how you feel when I say the word—maybe you can even feel sensations in your body. Just pay attention. It's okay to not feel anything—simply observe and be curious.

Happy.

Sad.

Excited.

Mad.

Stressed.

Bored.

Loving.

Anxious.

Worried.

Scared.

Disgusted.

Disappointed.

Jealous.

Quiet.

Surprised.

Silly.

Peaceful.

When you are done, ask how it felt. Was your child able to notice emotions? Remind her that whatever she experienced is okay. You can do all the emotions in one go or stop between each word and discuss it.

Emotion masks

Purpose: Understanding emotions, Emotional intelligence

Best for: Ages 4+, groups or one-on-one

What you need:

Construction Paper

Markers

Paper Plates

Craft Sticks (Optional)

Plastic googly eyes (Optional)

Yarn (Optional)

Decide what feelings you want to focus on. You can start with "Happy," "Sad," "Angry," and "Excited". For older children, design masks for each of the feelings you've chosen. For younger children, choose just one feeling at a time. After making a mask for each feeling, take a few minutes to talk about an example of when you each felt that way. If your child is struggling to think of an example, ask them when their closest friend felt that feeling or even when a character from their favorite TV show or movie experienced that feeling. Often, children have a much easier time understanding their own feelings when they can observe them in others.

This activity was kindly inspired by my child and family therapist friend, Michelle Paget, who has a private practice that focuses on building social emotional skills for children and families with the help of yoga and mindfulness. For more information about Michelle, you can visit her website at www.michellepagettherapy.com.

Recognizing emotions
Purpose: Understanding emotions, Emotional intelligence

Best for: Ages 4+, one-on-one

What you need: Nothing

This might seem too simple, but it is actually an important first step in teaching your child mindfulness. Of course your child recognizes his emotions when they are at extremes. But how does he recognize the feelings that lead up to the extremes?

You can help your child become aware of these subtle changes in mood and emotions. A good place to start is when your child is happy or content. Ask him how he is feeling, but take it further. Talk to him about how his body feels. When he is excited about an upcoming trip, ask him if he feels butterflies in his stomach or how his face feels when he can't stop smiling. Later, use this same technique when your child is upset. Ask him how his stomach feels, how the muscles in his body feel. Help him discover where in his body he physically feels emotions. As your child becomes tuned in to these subtle body changes, he will be able to recognize them before they reach an unpleasant extreme.

Kind and helpful

Purpose: Impulse control, Connection, Mindful speaking

Best for: Ages 5+, groups or one-on-one

What you need: Nothing

This activity helps children when they encounter a situation where they are not sure how to respond (mindfully), or they feel that they might say something unkind. The idea is that we simply ask ourselves two questions to check if what we are going to say is kind and helpful.

Tell your child that it's sometimes hard to be kind and helpful. Offer some examples (when angry, jealous, frustrated, etc.). Ask him if he has experienced something similar. Maybe he has said or done something that he later regretted? Why does he think he said it? If he said something unkind, how did the other kid respond? Explain that people tend to be kind to us if we're helpful and kind towards them. Next, tell him that he can ask himself two questions in those complicated situations to make sure he's kind and helpful.

Ask yourself:

The thing I am going to say …

1. Is it kind?
2. Is it helpful?

Role-play a few imaginary situations and let him ask the questions. Ask him to answer and help him out. With older children you may want to start with the Three Questions activity.

Emotion hunt

Purpose: Understanding emotions, Emotional intelligence, Connection

Best for: Ages 5+, groups or one-on-one

What you need: Nothing

Have a discussion about emotions and do the Trying Out Emotions activity to prepare your child for this one. At breakfast, ask your child to recognize at least one strong emotion today. Ask her to "catch" at least one strong emotion today. Tell her that you will ask her about it at dinner or just before bedtime. List a few possible emotions she might catch. Strong emotions like anger, joy, sadness, and excitement are pretty easy to notice.

Later that day, ask her about her day and her feelings. Was she able to catch a strong emotion at some point during that day? What was it? How did it make her feel? Did it stay long? Did she feel the emotion in her body somewhere?

Sensing emotions

Purpose: Understanding emotions, Emotional intelligence, Connection

Best for: Ages 5+

What you need: Nothing

This activity is best used after you've tried both Trying Out Emotions and Emotion Hunt. Ask your child to catch a few strong emotions today and to tell you about it. List a few possible emotions she might catch. Strong emotions like anger, joy, sadness, and excitement are pretty easy to notice.

Tell her that this time you want her to pay close attention to the emotion and see if she can feel it somewhere in her body as it happens. Give her examples. A sensation like "butterflies" in her tummy when she's happy. Maybe she can feel something in her face and tummy when she's angry.

Later that day, ask her about her day and if she was able to catch and inspect emotions. Was she able to notice a sensation in her body when she experienced a strong emotion? Remember that any outcome is okay. If she did notice emotions, then ask what the emotion was and how it felt. Where did she feel it exactly? Finally, ask her if she thinks it's useful to notice emotions like this? How could it help her?

Snuggle more

Purpose: Emotional intelligence, Connection

Best for: Ages 5+, one-on-one

What you need: Nothing

How often do you hug? It's the simplest way to connect. It's a skill and you can train to hug more. Sometimes a hug can make a huge difference to a child who is anxious, sad or upset. A hug can trigger your child to open up and talk about whatever is on her mind.

Cuddling with your child is fun (they even make these cute noises when you do it). Scientists say it's good for your health too—that cuddling promotes happiness and lowers stress hormones. Physical affection can help the brain, the heart and other body systems. Go ahead and go hug your kid (for no reason), and ask them how it makes them feel. Tell them that you love it.

You can obviously do this with your spouse too. Try hugging your spouse every day for at least 20 seconds, for a full week. Make the hugs long and see how it makes you feel. It's a great way to model affection at home.

Happy place - a guided visualization
Purpose: Calm, Relaxation

Best For: Ages 5+, groups or one-on-one

What you need: Nothing

Use visualization and your creative imagination to make this fun for everyone. Visualization is one of the easier ways to ease children into meditation.

Take turns being the one who gets to suggest an imaginary setting. "I'm thinking of a cabin in the woods," "I'm picturing myself on a tropical island," "I'm in a pasture with some really sweet horses," or "I'm floating in a hot air balloon."

Then close your eyes and experience the scene together in silence. Go through all of your five senses and imagine the experience completely. If you like, you can talk about your experiences afterwards, enjoying one another's imagined scenes. You can use the following script with your child or you can rehearse it a few times and make it your own:

Guided script:
Imagine a scene that brings you comfort. It may be your bedroom with all of your favorite toys. It may be a place you have visited before, like the beach, or a cabin in the woods.

Imagine how it sounds there.

How do you feel there, warm... cool... comfortable?

What smells do you notice?

What do you see in your mind as you look around you?

Sit for a moment and enjoy this place of comfort.

Take all the time that your child needs to explore her scene and be patient as she expresses what she is experiencing. It can be difficult for children to translate visualization into the reality of the spoken word, at least in terms that you might be expecting. Take this opportunity to explore the beauty of your child's world with her.

Cloud spotting
Purpose: Emotional regulation, Calm

Best For: Ages 6+, groups or one-on-one

What you need: Nothing

Start with a minute or even just 30 seconds. You can use the following script with your child, or you can rehearse it a few times and make it your own.

Guided script:
Imagine your mind as the vast, blue sky.

Envision your thoughts as white, fluffy clouds that appear, linger, and then pass by.

Each time a thought pops into your mind, as thoughts tend to do, allow it to drift by and then disappear, just as a cloud in the sky would do.

When ready, ask the child how it felt and what she noticed during the session. And if there's a difference in how she feels afterwards.

Idea jar
Purpose: Emotional regulation, Calm

Best for: Ages 6+, groups or one-on-one

What you need: A jar and pieces of paper

When difficult emotions become too much to handle, pay a visit to the "idea jar." What are the best ways for you to calm down and relax? Maybe yoga stretches help you calm down. Perhaps drawing is soothing for you. Write your ideas down on pieces of paper and put them in a jar. When difficult emotions become too much to handle, pay a visit to the "idea jar."

This jar should be filled with strips of paper with brief, calming activities written on them. Keep the jar in a quiet place in your home with a large, soft cushion nearby. Then draw a piece of paper out of the jar and complete the activity. Here are some activity ideas:

- Sit and take five calm breaths
- Prepare and sip a cup of tea (with parental help)

- Color a mandala, or work on your coloring book
- Do a tree pose on each side
- Recall a happy memory
- Think of three things you are grateful for

Color breathing

Purpose: Emotional regulation, Calm

Best for: Ages 6+, groups or one-on-one

What you need: Nothing

Before using this strategy, your child needs to be able to associate specific colors with specific emotions (e.g., red=anger, green=jealousy, blue=peaceful, yellow=happy). For younger children, it may help to have a discussion (or drawing session) that focuses on how colors can represent feelings prior to using this strategy. Older children and teenagers may be able to associate emotions with specific colors independently without a prior discussion or activity.

Introduce this exercise when your child is calm. Later, when you sense that your child is experiencing a moment of frustration, ask her to pause for a moment, close her eyes, and picture a color. Ask her what color she sees and if she can connect the color with her current emotions. Ask her how she feels. After your child responds, let's say for instance that she is feeling "red," instruct her to close her eyes and breathe in a color that relaxes her. Common relaxing colors are blue, pink, purple, and white, but it can be any color that your child associates with calm and peaceful emotions. Have her count to five as she inhales.

If your child chose blue for her calm color, have her inhale the blue air for a count of five. Then instruct her to exhale the "red" air and send it away from her body. Continue the process, encouraging her to inhale and exhale deeply, bringing in the color associated with the positive emotion while sending away the color associated with negativity and frustration. Ask your child if there's a difference in how she feels afterwards.

7 and up

Emotional check-in

Purpose: Noticing and understanding emotions, Emotional intelligence

Best for: Ages 7+, groups or one-on-one

What you need: Nothing

This activity will help your kid to get in touch with their emotions. The more they practice, the easier it will get. Think of a place or a task at home that can act as a trigger – a reminder to check in on emotions. It could be the act of washing hands or touching the bathroom doorknob or the fridge or spotting a painting. Then ask your kid to do an emotional check-in every time they encounter the trigger. Every time they wash their hands (for example), ask them to pause, take a deep breath, and ask themselves "How am I feeling?" Ask your kid to answer themselves too, even if it feels silly. A detailed answer will help them more than a generic "I feel fine."

Depending on the trigger, this emotional check-in can be something they do once or a few times per day. You can even make a game of it and ask them, at the end of the day, how many times they were able to check in.

Remember to ask them how this activity makes them feel, too. If it's helpful for them. Checking in on our emotions can help us make changes before emotions escalate. The more we understand how we're feeling, the more we can do something about it.

Name it to tame it

Purpose: Noticing and understanding emotions, Emotional intelligence

Best for: Ages 7+, one-on-one

What you need: Nothing

Emotions can be like wild beasts. Sometimes they are right in your face, growling, and sometimes they hide, ready to pounce. When we notice that we are, in fact, experiencing emotions, we can learn to focus, calm down, and reflect before we take action.

When feeling angry, sad, scared, excited, and even bored, don't just feel it. Name it! That's the mental component. Once the emotion is called out, we can zoom in to the physical to see how and where that feeling shows up in our bodies. Before becoming outraged, for example, you feel tension in your body, your heart rate increases, and you either stop breathing or experience shallow breaths. You probably feel like you're about to explode. This goes for all intense emotions. As we get better at detecting our feelings, we can more quickly notice when they're present (or on the way) and decide how we want to respond versus just reacting without much thought.

Example: I notice that I'm feeling anxious, so, in my mind, I say "anxious." Then I pay attention to my body and realize the discomfort in my stomach, the tightness in my chest, tension in my shoulders, and the whole heavy-headed feeling. This is often enough to help me accept whatever is going on inside of me, and I can move on to do something to get a fresh perspective. I could, for example, decide to stop and breathe mindfully for a minute.

In this one act, you and your child can break away from a stressful situation, even for a moment.

The way you can help your kid is to guide them through this simple activity when you notice them struggling.

1. Simply ask them to pause for a while and see if they can name the emotion they are experiencing.
Ask them how they feel—what it feels like in their body. Ask them what emotion that could be.

2. Then continue to discuss where it could lead if they weren't aware of the emotion building up. How being nervous can lead to stress building up, and how that could result in anger, for example.

Thought buses
Purpose: Mindfulness of thoughts, Calm

Best For: Ages 7+, groups or one-on-one

What you need: Nothing

Spend a minute just observing your thoughts. You can use the following script with your child, or you can rehearse it a few times and make it your own.

Guided script:
Imagine you are sitting on a bench near a busy road.

You are watching the buses pass by.

You can think of your thoughts as buses that lead you to specific moods and thought patterns. You don't have to jump on the bus, you just watch it arrive and drive by, disappearing down the road. Just wave goodbye as it passes.

Now, spend a minute noticing your thoughts.

Try to let them go past like the buses.

Whatever happens is okay.

When ready, ask the child how it felt and what she noticed during the session. And if there's a difference in how she feels afterwards.

Once your child becomes familiar with this activity, have her recognize thoughts that are frustrating. It is normal for these things to come into our lives. What we can learn to do is to recognize and let go of them. We let them drive by and disappear down the road, instead of transporting us to places like Worryville or Sadness City.

The idea is not to stop thinking or to ignore your thoughts but to recognize thoughts for what they are and avoid automatically falling into negative thought patterns. With a calm mind, we are better equipped to deal with whatever it is that is troubling us. Enjoy the process and see if the time between buses gets longer as you practice. A bus may pass by every few seconds instead of every second. Enjoy the silence between buses.

One line a day
Purpose: Understanding emotions, Emotional intelligence

Best for: Ages 8+, groups or one-on-one

What you need: A notebook and pen

Many children have difficulty pinpointing why they feel certain emotions. To help your child understand the cause behind her feelings, consider encouraging her keep a "one line a day" emotion journal.

Before you begin, help your child come up with a long list of feelings. Most children will say the simple ones: happy, sad, scared, angry, etc. Talk with her about more complex emotions such as jealousy, confusion, excitement, and apprehension. An older child may be able to come up with a list of emotions on her own. Keep the list at the front or back of her one-line-a-day notebook – or somewhere else that is easily accessible.

Then, show her how to record what she's feeling in her one-line-a-day notebook; she can refer to her list to help determine which emotion she is currently experiencing and record it. Since this activity should be easy to do, it will probably help to give her a sentence starter. For example, you might start her off with "I feel _____ because _____." The "because" part is important: the exercise is designed to help her reflect on the why of her feelings. She can use the same sentence starter every day.

This is a fantastic ritual for the evening when the child has had experiences throughout the day to reflect upon.

12 and up

Listening to thoughts and music
Purpose: Noticing and understanding thoughts, Emotional intelligence

Best for: Ages 12+, groups or one-on-one

What you need: Music

Show your kids how to sit and reflect with certain music. The style of music that helps each person come to a place of mindfulness is highly individual, so it is important to respect that. Ask your kid to spend ten minutes in the morning just listening to music and focusing on the direction of their thoughts. Afterwards, ask them what they noticed.

Emotion detectives

Purpose: Understanding emotions, Emotional intelligence

Best for: Ages 12+, groups or one-on-one

What you need: Nothing

Most of us have some amount of warning before we experience a big emotion. As we start to become better "emotion detectives," we can recognize the warning signs of big emotions coming. When we notice emotions we can name the emotion we are experiencing to help take its power away. When we observe our inner life like this we can more readily prevent coming meltdowns.

Try out Trying Out Emotions, Emotion Hunt, and Sensing Emotions to prepare for this game.

Play emotion detectives with your child for a day or two. Tell your child that the next time she experiences a difficult emotion, she should try to name it. Sometimes it's easy, at other times she might not notice it until after. She might get angry and say something she later wishes she didn't.

Tell her to catch anger, anxiety, sadness or something more subtle and elusive like jealousy and boredom—and to name the emotion when she feels it. Tell her that paying attention to and naming the emotion can take its power away. Ask her to see if she can figure out what sensation goes with what emotion when she notices the emotion.

It might look like this:
"I'm anxious."

"My stomach is tense."

Ask her about her day and the feelings she noticed during that day, at dinner or before bedtime for the course of your game. Ask her if she was able to notice and name emotions, and if that changed her mood. Did it allow her to respond better? Did she feel like she had a choice to act more skilfully when someone or something pushed her buttons? Did it help her to stay cool?

Finally, tell her that when we feel ourselves becoming frustrated or overwhelmed, we can practice mindfulness (e.g. taking slow mindful breaths) to further calm our minds.

Talk with family and friends
Purpose: Understanding emotions, Emotional intelligence, Connection

Best for: Ages 12+, one-on-one

What you need: Nothing

This may sound too simple, but it's really important to help your kid learn to talk to you or a friend when they are feeling down. Help them use their words to talk about how they feel and why they feel it. Holding in our feelings is painful, and may allow bigger issues to grow unattended. Explain this to your kid and show him the benefits of talking it out.

I used to try to hide my feelings before realizing that this wasn't something I wanted my son to learn from me because hiding our feelings usually only makes it worse—and kids pick up on our moods anyway. I still practice how to share my feelings more openly with my family.

Three questions
Purpose: Impulse control, Mindful speaking, Connection

Best for: Ages 12+, groups or one-on-one

What you need: Nothing

Three Questions is a smart exercise. We simply ask ourselves three questions to check if what we are going to say is kind, necessary and helpful. With younger children you may want to start with Kind And Helpful, which is very similar but uses just two questions in a similar manner.

Explain that sometimes, especially when our buttons are pushed, we react without thought and can hurt the feelings of others. Ask your child if he has ever said something he has regretted? Perhaps something that hurt someone else. Tell him that it happens to everyone, but even if we are in an argument we can be kind and helpful. And that being helpful in an argument often times helps to resolve the whole thing. The other party will listen to us more closely when we are constructive, kind and helpful—which in turn will lead to a quicker resolution.

Ask your child if he can remember a time when it was hard for him to decide how to respond. Recall a few personal examples of a time when you could have been more kind and helpful. You can prepare a few examples, either imaginary or real to test the questions with.

Investigate if the response is respectful by asking these questions:
1. Is it true?
2. Is it kind?
3. Is it necessary?

After you have practiced discernment, tell him to ask himself the three questions the next time he thinks he might not be that respectful towards others—when in an argument or when people gossip, for example. It's okay if he remembers just one of the questions, that will help him too. Even the simple act of pausing to think may hold back unkind words.

Mindful writing

Purpose: Understanding emotions, Emotional intelligence

Best for: Ages 12+, groups or one-on-one

What you need: A pen, a journal

Writing is a great way to teach your child to explore feelings. Explain to your child that it's sometimes hard to work our problems inside ones' head and that writing about emotions can help them to work through problems (like when they experience problems with a friend). Let your child pick out a journal they like and a special pen for it.

Sample writing prompts:
Write the words you'd like to most hear right now.

Write the words you don't like to hear.

Make a list of 25 things that makes you smile.

Write "I feel" at the top of your paper then write for five minutes.

I feel happiest when...

I feel sad when...

I feel uncomfortable when...

I get angry when...

The inner critic

Purpose: Understanding emotions, Emotional intelligence

Best for: Ages 12+, groups or one-on-one

What you need: Pen and paper

Explain to your kid that we can be our own harshest critics. Our minds tend to think about worst-case scenarios, and this negative, fear-based thinking affects our moods. When we get to know our "inner critic," we can dismiss his nagging voice when it's useful for us.

Tell your child to do a "Top 10 List" of his inner critics' most popular rants—negative thinking that he has noticed that he repeats. You can do it together and you may want to give some examples of your own.

"I'll never finish this mindfulness activity book."

"People will hate the book, even if I somehow finish it."

"No one will buy it, and I will run out of money to finance my mindfulness blog."

Or ...
"I'll never ace the exam, I failed the last time too."
"My friends will think I'm stupid when I fail the test."

"I will never get into college like this."

"My parents will be crazy furious."

Explain that, most of our fears never happen, and dwelling on fear-based imaginary stories is counterproductive. So instead of spending ten minutes worrying about my book, I could calm my mind and actually do some writing. Or ask for study help or just study some more to get confident.

Next, go through the Top 10 List and discuss the items. Most items are likely fear-based thoughts. Tell him that the next time he notices his inner critic, he can practice his ABCs To Calm The

Inner Critic found in the next activity. You may want to role-play a few different scenarios based on his Top 10 list too.

ABCs to calm the inner critic

Purpose: Noticing and acknowledging emotions, Emo-tional intelligence

Best for: Ages 12+, groups or one-on-one

What you need: Pen and paper

When you notice your inner critic complaining, pause and do the following in your mind:

Acknowledge the critic: "Howdy, there you are again—I see you."

Be kind to yourself, instead of engaging with the critic.

Create a space of positivity by listing three things you are thankful for and/or three things you like about yourself.

This way, you can find your center and calm your mind to make a skillful decision on how to change course.

Mindful friends

Purpose: Emotional intelligence, Mindful listening, Focus

Best for: Ages 12+, groups or one-on-one

What you need: Someone to listen to

Explain how mindfulness is about connecting with other people too—about paying attention to them. Do you want to improve a relationship? Learn to pay attention. Being a compassionate listener deepens our relationship and connection with others. The ability to pay attention to our friends and loved ones with kindness, without instantly judging them, is worth gold.

How does it make you feel when someone plays with their phone when you are trying to connect with them? Can you remember when someone was curious about something you told them? How did it make you feel? Was it comforting? Did you feel appreciated, even special? How does it feel to give this type of attention to someone else? If someone talks to you and you're only hearing but not listening, you miss the opportunity to connect.

Ask your kid to give special attention to one person today. It could be a sibling, a friend, a special someone or even a parent. Tell your kid to really listen without judging—without a snappy comeback, a joke or instantly making it about themselves. Ask them to listen and to ask further questions and to see how this special attention makes them and the other person feel.

Mindful testing

Purpose: Reduce test anxiety, Mindfulness of thoughts and emotions, Calm

Best For: Ages 12+, groups or one-on-one

What you need: Nothing

Explain that we sometimes experience difficult emotions when faced with tests, and that when we are able to deal with those emotions we can perform better. We may experience these difficult feelings because we want to do well in the test.

Ask your child to try mindful breathing just before a test, for a great start, or during a test, to focus, calm down, and perform better. Role-play the situation a few times with the help of a short visualization to make it easier for your child to do when he needs it.

Tell your child that he doesn't have to see anything, just imagine that he is part of the story you will tell him. Ask your child to sit still, close his eyes, and imagine that he is taking a test.

Guided script:
Imagine yourself on the day of the test.

You are sitting on your chair with the test paper in front of you with a pen in your hand.

You feel a little excited, and the test is going well.

Notice how that makes you feel.

Then you come across a question that is really hard.

You know you've read about it, but you can't remember the answer.

Pay attention to how you feel now.

Are you nervous? Are you anxious?

These feelings can affect the rest of the test too, once you becomes nervous like this.

But it's okay, you can help your mind calm down and focus.

Imagine that you put your pencil down.

You close your eyes in the fantasy.

Take a deep breath and slow down.

Breathe in slowly, and breathe out slowly.

Take three more deep breaths, and as you do so, see if you can feel your breath at your nose, chest or belly.

See if you can feel your belly go up and down as you breathe slowly.

Take two more slow breaths, then notice if you can feel your feet.

Bring your full attention to the soles of your feet by pushing them softly against the ground for a short moment.

Pay attention to your feet.

Feel how they make contact with the ground.

How does it feel? Soft or hard?

Can you feel your socks or your shoes?

Can you feel the chair supporting you?

Take one more deep breath.

You open your eyes in the fantasy.

You feel calmer, and your mind feels clear.

Now, when you look at the question again, your mind is calm, and the answer will come to you more easily.

You continue to do the test calmly, and when you finish, you feel satisfied.

You are now finished, and you hand in your test.

Enjoy the feeling of success.

When you are ready, tell your child that he can do the same exercise before and during a test to reduce test anxiety.

Troubleshooting

I'm pretty sure you will not need this, but here's a link to an article I wrote (and like to update) on troubleshooting with some examples of how to deal with difficulty. How to respond when kids say things like

"I'm bored."

"I don't like it."

"It doesn't work."

"It's stupid."

"I can't do it."

"It's not worth the time."

And so on.

You can find the article online here: www.blissfulkids.com/umab/

Share Your Favorite Activity with the World

We plan to continue to share more mindfulness activities with the world. That's what we do. Please let us know if you'd like to share your favorites with us. You can email me at: christian at blissfulkids dot com

More Mindfulness for Kids, Teens, and Grown-ups

Sign up to my newsletter for more inspiration, books, online courses, and free mindfulness activities.

Sign up here: www.blissfulkids.com/sign-up/

Our Online Mindfulness Courses

I recommend POSITIVE MINDFULNESS FOR KIDS AND TEENS.

It's all about integrating mindfulness step-by-step to boost joy, focus, kindness, and calm. You'll learn four essential core mindfulness techniques in-depth: gratitude practice, loving kindness practice, appreciative joy practice, and mindful breathing.

What's great is that you learn a variety of ways to practice each core technique. The secret sauce in this course is that you'll have many different ways to practice. The course is really about building a powerful toolkit. By the end of the course, you'll know 10-15 different ways to practice. With varying degrees of ease. So that you can mix different ways to practice. To combat boredom. Yeah, kids get easily bored too. And... so that you'll have a quick and easy way to practice even when you're busy or having a tough day (because that's when you need practice most). This variety and ease will translate to a fun, sustainable practice.

The best part is that you and the kids will learn mindfulness tools for life: activities to make you feel better and exercises that will help you to connect with each other. Each activity is practical, easy, and quick to do. All activities can be easily integrated into a busy schedule at home or at school. And we show you exactly how. It's all very uncomplicated and practical. And easy to integrate into your routines.

This course makes it super easy for you to get started and helps to refresh and deepen your skills if you're already a practitioner.

Learn the techniques in-depth and gain the confidence and skills you need to sustain a successful practice with kids and youth. Start practicing with your family or class today!

Sign up here: www.blissfulkids.com/courses/

ABOUT THE AUTHOR

Chris Bergstrom, is the founder of BlissfulKids.com, a blog dedicated to children's mindfulness, and a dad who is thrilled to practice mindfulness with his son. He is a certified mindfulness facilitator and trained to teach mindfulness to students in K-12. He's also an executive consultant and has taught meditation for more than 15 years.

Urgent Plea!

Thank you for downloading our book! We really appreciate all of your feedback, and we love hearing what you have to say.

We need your input to make the next version better.

Please leave us a helpful REVIEW on Amazon.

Thanks so much!!

Chris Bergstrom

INDEX

Activities for Sensory Awareness, Focus and Calm
3 and up

7 and up

12 and up

Mindful Breathing
3 and up

Activities for Joy, Gratitude, and Kindness
3 and up

Made in the USA
Middletown, DE
21 August 2019